MW01290428

The world of Cajsa Andersdotter

A close-up view of Sweden in the 18th and 19th century

Bengt Hällgren

Title of the Swedish original:
Cajsa Andersdotters värld - En närbild av Sverige
på 1700- och 1800-talet

Translated to English by
Bengt Hällgren, Carol Hällgren, and Amy Frankel

Cover illustration by
Carol Hällgren

© Bengt Hällgren, 2017

Production: CreateSpace Independent Publishing Platform

ISBN-13: 978-1977635501
ISBN-10: 1977635504

Contents

Preface

Dear reader,

Growing up during the 1950's and 60's, my sister, Ingrid Häll-gren Skoglund, and I often visited our maternal grandparents, Carl and Elin Nyman, in Trollhättan. Elin taught us things like lighting a fire in the woodstove, making hash, or cooking a compote of gooseberries. Besides such practical skills, she gladly sang old folk songs and told us stories from her childhood.

Elin was born in 1888, and as a child and teenager she had, in her turn, spent much time with her grandmother, Cajsa Anders-dotter. Thus, Elin told us what Cajsa had told her about events that had occurred already during the first half of the 19th century. Later, after we had grown up and Elin wasn't there anymore to answer our questions, we began to ponder over Cajsa's stories. Had she really served the king a glass of water? And why did she refuse to reveal anything about her childhood? These questions prompted us to search the old Church Registers in order to map out Cajsa's life, but in the 1970's, this kind of searches were not easy. The documents were photographed in black and white on rolls of microfilm that could only be ordered no more than five at a time from a central archive. Microfilm scanners were available at the local city library, but viewing options were restricted to the hours of the library's daily operating schedule. During the 19th century, poor young people in the countryside, such as Cajsa and our other relatives, worked as farmhands and maids and generally sought new employment every year, which meant that they moved from farm to farm and sometimes from parish to parish. In order to keep track of them, we had to order new microfilms repeatedly and sometimes even wait for the films to become available. Thus, it could take weeks to trace the next move of Cajsa or some other relative. Finally, we gave up on this tedious project, and the binder, containing the collected data, ended up in a far corner of a bookshelf.

But the years go by fast, and when we retired earlier this decade, we made a new attempt to verify Cajsa's stories. Now it proved to be much easier. For a relatively modest yearly fee, one can access online not only the Church Registers but a great number of other documents. No longer confined by the city library's opening hours, one can sit at ease in front of one's own computer. The waiting time to receive a specific register or document, which during the 1970's could be weeks, is now reduced to a few seconds. *ArkivDigital* has photographed the documents in color, which makes them easier to read, and even the *Swedish National Archives* has made much of their material accessible via the Internet. The combination of available documents makes it possible to find a surprising amount of personal data even about poor and humble ancestors. The aim of genealogical research, therefore, is no longer limited to creating a family tree with mere names and dates of births and deaths but can develop into complete stories about people who lived generations ago.

During the history lessons at school in the 1960's, we memorized the succession of Swedish kings and the years of their reign, studied a number of wars, including the locations and dates of important battles, and learned what land areas Sweden gained or lost in the peace agreements. This book offers a close-up view of Swedish history from about 1760 to 1910, seen from a totally different perspective. The story is based on documented facts about Cajsa Andersdotter's family, and illustrates how poverty, starvation, disease, and helplessness dominated the life of ordinary people. However, Cajsa Andersdotter's story also forebodes an emerging change within the Swedish society from government control and social segregation towards democracy and equality. My sister, Ingrid, who has taught history and Swedish all of her professional life, has helped me realize how the decisions of the ruling class influenced the situation of common people. As a result, this perspective has become an essential part of my book. To help the reader become familiar with the overall history of Sweden, among the supplements, I have enclosed a timeline with kings/queens and wars. I have also included a series of maps illustrating the country's changing borders.

During the 18th and 19th century, it was not uncommon for families to have five or even ten children. Therefore, the number of names you encounter as you read about Cajsa Andersdotter's family line may seem overwhelming. To make it easier for you to focus on Cajsa's, and later our grandmother Elin Nyman's, *direct forefathers*, who form the backbone of the story, their names are printed in *italics*.

If you, dear reader, discover any mistakes in my book or happen to have further information which can complement my text, don't hesitate to contact me.

Sincerely,

Bengt Hällgren

bengt@haellgren.se

Introduction

Driving southward down the road E45 through the province of Dalsland, for a long time you see mostly hills covered with spruce forest. Shortly before Mellerud, however, the landscape opens up, and you enter a flatland called Dalsboslätten. There, wide fields of fertile farmland extend on both sides of the road, with a few farm houses spread out among them. Nowadays, only 15 % of Sweden's population lives in rural areas, since modern, mechanized agriculture requires few working hands. In the 18th and 19th centuries, the situation was quite different. The tractor was still unknown, and many hands were needed to assist with farming. In the beginning of the 19th century, as much as 90 % of Sweden's population lived in the countryside. Horse and cart was the fastest means of traveling, until the first railroad through Dalsland opened in 1879. It ran from Kil to Öxnered, about 160 kilometers, and soon both trade and transports spread to the towns that sprang up around the railroad stations. Nowadays, most people prefer to drive rather than take the train, but the route through Dalsland is almost the same, since the E45 runs along the railroad southward through Mellerud, Erikstad, Brålanda and Frändefors.

However, there is also another road that runs across the plain of Dalboslätten. It turns east from the E45, just north of Mellerud, and passes the churches in Holm, Järn, Grinstad, Bolstad, Gestad and Timmervik, before it merges into the E45 again, north of Vänersborg. It is easy to understand why this road must be very old. The churches in Holm, Järn and Grinstad were built in the 13th century. The church in Bolstad is even older, probably dating back to the middle of the 12th century. In Gestad, where this story begins, the population outgrew its 13th century church. Thus, during the last years of the 18th century, a new church was built on a hill 400 meters south of the old one. The church in Timmervik, which also belongs to the parish of Gestad, was built as late as 1927.

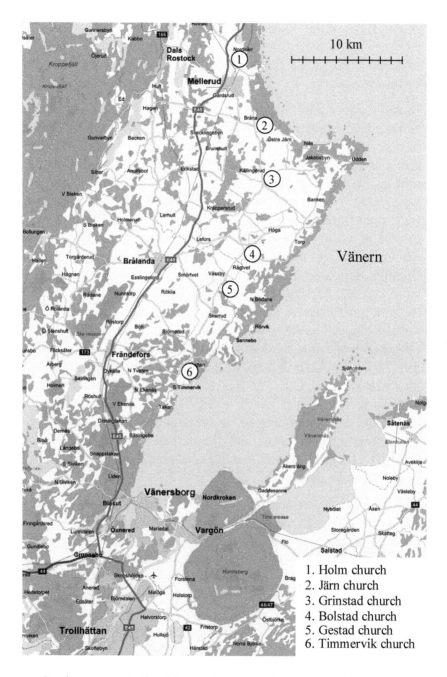

10 km

Vänern

1. Holm church
2. Järn church
3. Grinstad church
4. Bolstad church
5. Gestad church
6. Timmervik church

Southeastern part of Dalsland and northwestern part of Västergötland.
Detail from Eniro's present-day map of Sweden.[1]

In the 18th and 19th centuries, the Church played a central role, not only in the parish, but also in the life of the parishioners. To understand how it reached that position, we'll glance back a little further in history.

In the 16th century, Sweden had split from the Catholic Church and adopted Lutheranism. Since then, it was no longer the Pope, but the Swedish king who headed the Church, and so the government and the Church could cooperate in steering the population in the direction they desired. To secure that all its subjects had accepted Lutheranism, in 1617, Parliament decided that all remaining Catholics must leave the country within three months or else they would be sentenced to expatriation or capital punishment. During the so-called Thirty Years War against the Catholic states in central Europe, further repressive measures were taken. The 1634 Instrument of Government stated that all Swedes must be members of the Church of Sweden, and attending the church services was made compulsory. Still, a concern remained that some individuals may hold heretic beliefs. Therefore, the 1686 Church Law stated that all clergy must hold annual hearings to make sure that their parishioners were able not only to recite Martin Luther's Small Catechism and Explanations, but also to understand its contents. Simultaneously, the clergy was instructed to check the parishioners' reading ability. Owing to this, the Swedish population acquired exceptional literacy rates already by the 18th century.

The hearings where the parsons tested the knowledge and abilities of their parishioners took on different forms. At the end of the 17th century, all parishes were divided up into files – groups of homesteads, each obliged to support one soldier for the army – and in the so-called File Catechetical Hearings, the parsons gathered their parishioners file by file. In the beginning, these hearings were held in church before or after the Sunday service. Furthermore, members of the parish who came to the parsonage on official business requesting, for example, the publication of banns or a relocation certificate, must also be prepared that the parson might test their knowledge of the catechism.[2]

In the first decades of the 18th century, King Charles XII waged a drawn-out war against Russia. Many Swedish soldiers ended up as prisoners of war in Siberia, where religion became their only comfort. Some of them returned home as devout Pietists, accustomed to leading meetings with prayer and readings from the Bible. The Church felt threatened by this movement, and in 1726 a law was passed that prohibited private religious meetings without the presence of an ordained clergyman. The same law stated that the annual Catechetical Hearings should be intensified to guarantee that no "false doctrines" had insinuated themselves into the population. The hearings were now held on the larger farms and documented in so-called Catechetical Hearing Registers. To make sure that all parishioners attended the hearings, beginning in 1765, fines were imposed on those who failed to appear. This accurate supervision of the parishioners' life and faith required that the clergy kept track of each individual who was born, married, lived and died in the parish. Thus, in addition to the Hearing Registers, other types of registers were gradually introduced: Birth and Baptism Registers, Wedding Registers, Relocation Registers, and Death and Funeral Registers. As an example, the first Catechetical Hearing Register in Gestad dates back to 1761, and the first copies of the other church registers to 1763.

With the rise of economic liberalism, urban migration, and of religious revivalism in the middle of the 19th century, people clamored for more lenient religious laws. As a result, in 1858 the law that had forbidden private religious meetings was revoked, and quitting the Church of Sweden became allowed on the condition that a person joined another Christian church approved by the government. Thus, people who were involved in the revivalist movements no longer had to migrate to America, but could practice their religion in Sweden. In 1888 compulsory attendance at Catechetical Hearings was revoked, but not until 1951 were Swedes allowed to quit the Church of Sweden, without having to join another religious community. However, the Church remained responsible for keeping registers of all citizens until 1991, when the Tax Authority took over this duty.

With hindsight, the power that the Church of Sweden once wielded over the population in the 18th and 19th centuries appears to have been oppressive. Nevertheless, the registration of all citizens offers a unique opportunity for modern Swedes to trace their roots back to the 18th century and, in some cases, even further into the past. The early registers are not quite complete, which makes it necessary to track each individual from register to register, from page to page, to make sure that you are following the right person. Common family names were not introduced until the beginning of the 20th century. Until then, individuals were given a last name consisting of their father's first name followed by the suffix -son or -daughter. Therefore, you will find a confusing number of people with the same names in the registers, which makes it important to identify the individuals you are looking for not only by their names, but also by their date of birth.

Chapter 1:

Cajsa Andersdotter's paternal ancestors

The farmer family who lost their estate

The story of *Cajsa Andersdotter's* paternal ancestors originates in a homestead called Simonstorp, which was located about one kilometer southeast of Gestad church. In those days farmland was divided into three categories depending on who owned it:

- gentry homesteads, which were owned by the nobility and thus exempt from taxes,
- taxed homesteads, which were owned by private farmers who were liable to pay taxes, and
- state homesteads, which were owned by the state and leased out to tenant farmers.

Gentry homesteads first appeared in the middle ages, when King Magnus Ladulås, in the year of 1280, decided that land owners who contributed to the army by supplying a fully equipped knight, would not have to pay taxes. This exemption from taxes was then inherited within the noble families. During the ensuing centuries, additional gentry homesteads were established, when the king granted land to noblemen as rewards for their efforts during the wars. However, the king could also confiscate land in

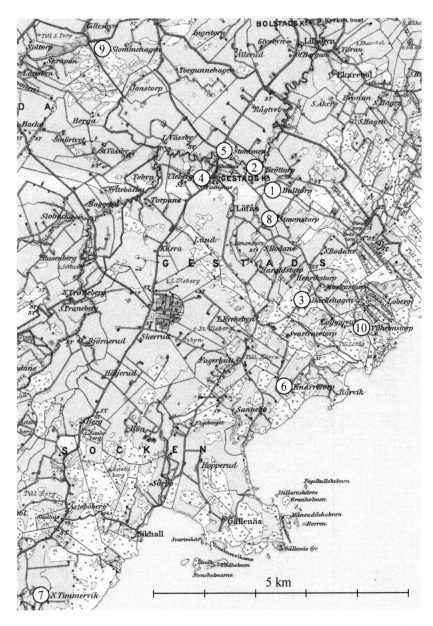

The parish of Gestad. Detail from map of Sundal judicial district 1895.[3]

1. Balltorp	5. Gestad soldier's croft	9. Slommehagen
2. Bröttorp	6. Knarretorp	10. Stenviken/
3. Bäckhagen	7. Norra Timmervik	Vilhelmstorp
4. Gestad church	8. Simonstorp	

so-called "reductions" which happened on a large scale during King Carl XI's reign at the end of the 17th century.

Taxed homesteads appeared in the 1620's, when Sweden's economy was heavily burdened by the war against the Catholic countries in the south of Europe. In order to increase the government's income, all citizens between 15 and 62 years of age were considered liable to pay taxes. Only the nobility, soldiers, and the impoverished were exempt. As a basis for the tax levy, special Tax Registers were established. In the beginning, tax collectors visited each home in a parish to collect necessary data, but this process changed over time. Eventually, tax collectors summoned the inhabitants of each file to annual meetings. Each summoned resident was then required to state the number of persons dwelling in his house (men, wives, children, elderly, farm hands, maids, dependent tenants etc.). Taxes were determined on this collected data. Today, genealogists use these old Tax Registers in addition to Church Registers for their research.

Because the homestead of Simonstorp was owned by private farmers, it was a taxed homestead. In the middle of the 18th century, it consisted of four farms and a soldier's croft, which was a house and a piece of land, supplied by the farmers of the file, to support a soldier, according to the so-called allotment system. From the Tax Registers, we can conclude that the first of the four farms of Simonstorp had been inherited from generation to generation, within the same family, beginning in the year 1682 or possibly even earlier. The information from the Tax Registers also indicates that the names of the owners had alternately been Segol Andersson and Anders Segolsson. In the first volume of Estate Inventories for the Judicial District of Sundal, covering the years 1736 to 1739, there is an inventory from 1737, when the farm Simonstorp no. 1 was inherited from the father, *Anders Segolsson*, to his son, *Segol Andersson*.[4] The document describes a fairly well-to-do estate, with a number of farm animals, including: a stallion and a mare with a foal, two oxen, a bull, six cows, three heifer, three calves, seven sheep, three lambs, three pigs, and two geese. The farmer had no debts, but assets are listed to 42 riksdaler [1] in cash, which was equivalent to the value of ten cows. For the farmland itself, no value is specified in the inventory. The heir, *Segol Andersson*, had three sisters with whom he was required to share the inheritance. Since sons in the countryside according to the national law of 1734 inherited twice as much as daughters, 2/5 of the value of the farm must have been awarded to *Segol*, while his sisters received 1/5 each. Most probably *Segol* had to raise a loan and sell some of the farm animals in order to be able to buy out his sisters and take over the farm himself.

In the very first Catechetical Hearing Register of Gestad, detailing the years 1761 to 1767,[5] we learn more about *Segol Andersson* of Simonstorp no. 1. He was born in 1714, and was married to a woman by the name of *Karin Bryngelsdotter*, born in 1720. Together, they had a number of children:

− Anders, born in 1745,

− Eric, born in 1751,

− *Olof*, born in 1753,

− Ingri, born in 1756,

− Johan, born in 1759,

− Jon, born in 1761, dead before the age of two, and

− Kerstin, born on July 4, 1763.[6]

The widow of the previous owner, *Anders Segolsson*, also lived on the farm. Her name was *Kerstin Jonsdotter*, and she was born in 1692. On January 9, 1763, she died of what was probably a stomach disease. *Kerstin Jonsdotter's* death was the very first death in Gestad Parish which was documented in the Death and Funeral Register of Bolstad Church District.[7] Six months later, the last of *Segol Andersson's* and *Karin Bryngelsdotter's* children was born, a daughter, who was given the name of her grandmother, Kerstin.

---

[1] Swedish currency before 1873.

On April 24, 1772, *Segol Andersson* died of tuberculosis,[8] and on August 14, two years later, his wife died of pneumonia.[9] Before his death, *Segol* had stipulated that the estate could not be divided up among his heirs until *Karin* had also passed away. Therefore, no estate inventory was made until after *Karin's* death. This inventory indicates that the condition of the estate had deteriorated significantly. The remaining animals had been reduced to one horse, five cows, two rams, twelve sheep, and one goose. Instead of cash assets, *Segol* had debts that totaled 253 riksdaler, equivalent to 28 % of the total value of the estate, including land. The inheritance was then further divided up in double shares for brothers over sisters, which meant that Anders, Eric, *Olof* and Johan each inherited 1/5 of the estate, whereas Ingri and Kerstin each received 1/10.[10] According to the Catechetical Hearing Register,[11] the oldest brother, Anders, proceeded to take over the farm. One asks oneself how this was possible, considering the fact that his siblings had the legal right to their share of the inheritance. Strangely enough, an explanation to this can be found thanks to a Parliamentary Resolution concerning agricultural reform.

Since medieval times, the land of Swedish farmers was separated into a number of smaller lots, located around the village where the farmers lived. The reason for this arrangement was the variation in the quality of the soil. In order to create a just distribution of land, each farmer was assigned a section of fertile ground, a section of meager ground, a section of forest ground etc. When several brothers and sisters later shared the inheritance of their parents, the sections were divided into increasingly smaller portions. After a number of generations, these portions were so small that they could no longer be tilled separately. In order to improve farming conditions, Parliament adopted several resolutions, stating that the land within the homesteads should be redistributed, so that each farmer possessed fewer but larger lots. The first of these resolutions, the so-called "great redistribution", was adopted in 1757. It stated that each farmer of a homestead had the right to request redistribution. The land surveyor would then compare and redistribute the lots. However, it was difficult to satisfy everybody, and those who found that they had been forced to trade superior lots for inferior ones, had the right to request a new redistribution. Sometimes, this occurred repeatedly. In 1827, Parliament imposed a final change, the so-called "legal redistribution". The purpose of this radical and permanent measure was that each farmer should be awarded one single, joint piece of land. At the same time, farmers were obliged to disperse the villages, in order to live adjacent to their fields in new farm houses subsidized by the government. One result of this change was the agricultural landscape which is visible today, where farm houses are distributed as single entities among the fields.

The first time the land surveyor was called to Simonstorp to perform a redistribution was on October 18, 1785. The accurately written minutes from this meeting [12] contain a map of the homestead (see map), the names of all the land owners, and a detailed description of their lots. This is where we can indirectly learn how the inheritance after Segol Andersson was divided up. Among the land owners listed in the meeting minutes, there is one who is not listed in the Catechetical Hearing Register as a resident of the homestead. His name is Erik Olsson, and he is the owner of Simonstorp no. 1, although he obviously neither lives there nor farms the land. According to the Catechetical Hearing Register, Anders Segolsson is the principle of Simonstorp no. 1, but he is not listed among the land owners in the minutes from the redistribution meeting. The only reasonable conclusion of this detail is that the Segolsson/Segolsdotter siblings must have been forced to sell their family estate, in order to share the inheritance. Subsequently, the oldest brother began farming the land as a tenant. Due to the numerous children of the two last generations, the family lost the estate which had been theirs for at least ninety years, and perhaps, even longer.

Segol Andersson remained the principle of Simonstorp no. 1 for eighteen years. Already before the death of his parents, he had married Botilla Andersdotter, born in Halland in 1745. Together, they had two children: Anders, born in 1772 [13] and Karin, born

Map of Simonstorp village from the great redistribution in 1785, infields included. The lots pertaining to Simonstorp no. 1 are marked with an A.

in 1775.[14] Aside from Ander's immediate family, his brothers Eric and Johan and his sisters, Ingri and Kerstin, also lived on the farm. His brother *Olof* was the only one who had moved away.[15] The Catechetical Hearing Register informs us that Anders Segolsson, just like his father, was appointed a juryman. Thus, he was a lay member of the District Court and participated in their meetings. The jurymen were appointed by the parish for a term of six years. Being a juryman was an honorable position and jurymen were regarded as important persons in the local community.

On March 9, 1788, Anders Segolsson's wife, Botilla, died of pneumonia.[16] Two years later, Anders passed away from a "mortal decease" at only 44 years of age.[17] His death was likely due to an epidemic of diphtheria, a highly contagious infectious disease, which had appeared in Stockholm in 1755 and consequently spread throughout the country. In the parish of Gestad, some thirty people, mostly children and elderly, died of diphtheria during the late winter of 1790. One of the symptoms of this disease was a gray, inflammatory coating of the tonsils, which may explain why the parson, in the first cases, specified "tonsillitis" as the cause of death. When the outbreak continued, and resulted in additional fatalities, he must have realized that this could not be the correct diagnosis, and thus shifted to simply writing "mortal disease."

The reserve soldier who disappeared

We will now leave the development at Simonstorp and go back a few years to trace Anders Segolssons younger brother *Olof Segolsson*, who would later become the grandfather of *Cajsa Andersdotter*. Unfortunately, the 18th century Catechetical Hearing Registers of Gestad rarely contain information about relocations. Thus, we do not know exactly when *Olof* left his parents' home in Simonstorp, but it most likely happened shortly after his father's death in 1774. If this is accurate, *Olof* would have been 21 years old, and was probably hired as a farmhand at one of the surrounding homesteads. Two years later, we find *Olof* working for Tolle Hansson, at Slommehagen no. 3, a farm located some four kilometers northwest of Simonstorp.[18] By this time, *Olof* is married to *Ingebor Halvardsdotter*, born in 1745. You may find it odd, that *Olof* choose a bride who was eight years older than himself, but this was not uncommon. During the first half of the 18th century, a great number of men had been sent to fight in King Karl XII's drawn out war against Russia. Many of them never returned, which gave rise to a surplus of women in Sweden. As a result, once a young man reached adult age, several women competed for his hand in marriage. This made it quite normal for young men to marry older women. Furthermore, population growth had made it increasingly difficult for young people to make a living, and without a secure position, it was hardly recommendable to start a family.[19] We do not know where *Ingebor* was born or where she and *Olof* were married. The couple is not listed in the Marriage Register of Gestad.

On February 28, 1778, *Ingebor* bore *Olof's* first child, a son named *Anders*, who would later become the father of *Cajsa Andersdotter*.[20] A short time thereafter, the family moved to Knarretorp, three kilometers south of Simonstorp.[21] There, on April 4, 1780, another child was born, a daughter, who received the name Britta.[22] Although we lost track of *Olof* between 1774 and 1776, we can now confirm that we are following the correct individual. Britta's godparents were *Olof's* brother, Eric Segols-son, of Balltorp, and the wife of his brother Anders, Botilla Andersdotter, of Simonstorp. Furthermore, *Olof* and *Ingebor* soon moved to his parents' homestead Simonstorp, where they were offered a home at the soldier's croft.

For us, who live more than two hundred years after *Olof* and *Ingebor*, it may not be clear what a soldier's croft was or to imagine what it might have resembled. In the late 17th century, King Karl XI had reformed the Swedish military. This resulted in the introduction of the so-called "new allotment system", which required that the parishes be divided up into files. The farmers of each file were obligated to set up a soldier for the army, by providing him with a cottage and a piece of land, sufficient in size to support him and his family. This was known as the soldier's croft. The cottage was generally built of timber and had a thatched roof. It contained an entrance, a kitchen which also served as living room and bedroom, and a closet. In Gestad, the parish was divided into six files, but in the 18th century it is obvious that the government had increased the demands on the farmers. According to the Catechetical Hearing Registers, each file now supported between two to five soldiers. All in all, the parish financed eighteen crofts, located on the bigger home-steads. When *Olof* and his family moved to Simonstorp, in the

Hearing Register a soldier named Lars Simongren was the first name of the croft. Therefore, it seems likely that *Olof's* family did not live in the very soldier's cottage, but in an adjoining hut. By the way, it is no coincidence that the name of the soldier, Simongren, makes us think of the name of the homestead, Simonstorp. In Gestad, the normal procedure seems to have been to name the soldiers after the homestead they served, adding a suffix like "-gren" (= branch) or "-dahl" (dal = valley). Thus, all soldiers who had been financed by the same homestead went under the same last name, despite the fact that they were not related.

But why did *Olof Segolsson* live at the soldier's croft if he was not a soldier? Did he have some other function in the Swedish military? In 1772, King Gustaf III seized the power from Parliament through a coup. He then began to mobilize the country's armed forces. As part of this plan, he ordered that all files, aside from the ordinary soldiers, recruit substitutes. A likely motive for this mobilization was to enable Sweden to regain the status it had possessed during the 17th century but later lost through the defeats of Karl XII. In 1787, the Ottoman Empire attacked Russia from the south in an effort to capture the Crimean Peninsula. Gustaf III took advantage of the situation. He ordered a land-based army, supported by the coastal navy, to march toward Russia, along the southern coast of Finland. At the same time, he let his open sea navy sail a second army directly toward the Russian capital of Saint Petersburg. However, the attack was not as successful as the king had hoped. On July 17, 1788, a Russian fleet encountered the Swedish sea navy near the island Hogland, in the Gulf of Finland. The battle lasted for six hours, but none of the parties gained the upper hand. The Swedish losses amounted to 300 dead and 850 men taken prisoner. Out of the soldiers from Gestad, who participated in the battle, two were killed in action, and four ended up as prisoners of war.[23] It is not clear if any of them eventually returned to their homes. However, it seems probable that the gaps they had left were filled by substitute soldiers.

Olof and *Ingebor* remained at the soldier's croft of Simonstorp through the 1780's.[24] On July 26, 1788, *Ingebor* bore another child, a daughter called Kerstin.[25] Her godparent's were two of *Olof's* siblings, his brother Eric and his sister Ingri. On September 28, baby Kerstin died at only two months of age, probably due to what would prove to be the beginning of an epidemic of smallpox.[26] The following year, the family moved one kilometer north to the soldier's croft of Bröttorp (or Bredtorp). There, the ordinary soldier, Nils Johansson Breddal, had been taken prisoner in the battle of Hogland. This time, we can be certain of *Olof's* military function, since the parson has entered "varjering", a word for reserve soldier, in the Catechetical Hearing Register.[27] After just a couple of months in the new homestead, *Olof's* family situation changed drastically. On January 10, 1790, his wife *Ingebor* died from a stomach disease.[28] Their children, who were now twelve and ten years old, became motherless.

It must have been difficult for a soldier to have the sole responsibility for a family, even if he was just a substitute. He had to practice shooting, combat, and drill, and was called to meetings with his company several days each month, in addition to meetings with his regiment two or three weeks each year. How was he then to take care of his children? The problem was solved by letting *Anders* and Brita move to live with their aunt Ingri Segolsdotter, who still resided at Simonstorp, with her husband, Erik Olofsson, and their three small children (another two had died at an early age). In their usual way, the family stuck together. Ingri's brother Johan Segolsson, his wife, and Ingri's sister Kerstin Segolsdotter, who was still single, all lived in the same house.

So what happened to *Olof Segolsson,* after his wife died, and his children moved out? In the Hearing Register 1787-95, the parson entered a note that *Olof* moved away from Bröttorp, but there is no indication of where, and Olof's name does not appear anywhere else in the same register. He may have moved to another parish, but this is difficult to confirm, since Relocation Registers were not kept in Gestad until 1806. Olof is not listed in the Military Register for the Västgöta-Dal Regiment from 1790 to 1798. It is possible that only ordinary soldiers were listed, not reserves. I have searched the Death and Funeral Register of Bolstad Church District between the years 1790 and 1800, without success. What happened to *Olof Segolsson*, thus, remains a mystery.

The man with the lame arm

As we already know, during most of the 1770's and 1780's, Simonstorp no. 1 was leased by the oldest of the Segolsson brothers, the juryman Anders Segolsson. Several of his siblings also remained at Simonstorp, but after Anders Segolsson's death in 1790, the land owner must have found another leaseholder. As a result, the siblings were separated. Ingri Segolsdotter and her family moved three kilometers southeast to a farm by the Lake Vänern called Stenviken, later renamed Vilhelmstorp. Even if information about moves in the early Hearing Registers of Gestad is incomplete and sometimes hard to interpret, we know for sure that they moved between 1794 and 1798. This can be confirmed by the place and date of birth of their children, as stated in Gestad Birth and Baptism Register.[29] Ingri's nephew, *Anders,* and niece, Brita, which she had been housing since their mother's death, also moved. Brita, now 15 years old, probably found a position as a maid in some farm. The name of the farm to which she moved is recorded in the Hearing Register, but the writing is difficult to interpret. Contrary to Britas new home, the name of the farm to which *Anders* moved is very clearly documented: "Stenviken 1796",[30] and indeed, in the next register, *Anders* turns up at Stenviken together with his aunt's family.

Why is it so important to present evidence that *Anders Olsson* moved to Stenviken with Ingri Segolsdotter's family? There was another Anders Olsson, also born in Gestad in 1778 which can confuse the picture. This Anders Olsson was the son of a soldier named Olof Olsson Silfverdahl of Norra Timmervik. Like his fellow soldier from Bröttorp, he had become as a prisoner of war in Russia, following the battle of Hogland. His son, Anders, stayed with his mother until he disappeared around 1796 without any information about where he might have moved. How can we be sure that he is not the Anders Olsson, who turns up at Stenviken, and later becomes the father of *Cajsa Andersdotter*? Evidence exists that refutes this hypothesis.

Anders, from Simonstorp, moved to Stenviken around the same time as his aunt's family. The loyalty among members of this extended family has been consistently demonstrated. After aunt Ingri had taken over the responsibility for her nephew and niece, *Anders* had remained living with her for six years. Despite the fact that he is now 18, he is identified as "boy", not "farmhand", in the Hearing Register. This indicates that *Anders* lived at Stenviken as a member of the family, rather than as an employee. In the same register, we learn that *Anders* suffered from a physical disability. He is described as "frail and lame in the right arm and quite disabled".[31] This explains why his aunt, Ingri, continued to care for him, even though he had now reached an age, when young people at that time normally supported themselves. Based on this evidence, we can be fairly certain that it was this *Anders* from Simonstorp, and not the Anders from Norra Timmervik, who would eventually become the father of *Cajsa Andersdotter*.

Ingri Segolsdotter and her family remained at Stenviken for five years. During this time she bore another child, but in August of 1799, two of her children died of pneumonia in the span of just one week.[32] In 1801, the family moved to Bäckehagen, one kilometer northwest of Stenviken, with two of the originally six children still alive.[33] The following year, they continued the remaining two kilometers to Simonstorp, where they were registered as domestic servants. It is here, in Simonstorp, that Ingri's husband died in 1807. Following his death, the children moved away, and Ingri continued on alone.[34]

So what happened to *Anders Olsson*, her disabled nephew? When his aunt's family left Stenviken, he was 23 years old and probably felt that it was time for him to prove that he could take care of himself, even though he had only one good arm. He was initially hired as a farmhand by their neighbor, Johan Larsson, at

Stenviken, but already in the same year, he moved to another farm, located next to the newly built Church of Gestad.[35] This farm belonged to the church and was leased to a tenant whose rent helped support the local parson. *Anders* remained at this location for five years, working as the only servant in a family with four young children. Not until now did *Anders* pass the Catechetical Test to be admitted to Holy Communion.[36] This may seem late for a man of 25, but at the time, it was not unusual. In order to be admitted, as proof of being an orthodox Lutheran, one must be able to read aloud from Luther's Small Catechism and be familiar with its contents. Teaching the children to read was primarily a responsibility of the parents. If the young people still could not read when they started work, it was the duty of their master to teach them. Finally, it was up to the pastor to confirm the reading ability and the orthodox belief of his parishioners. In 1811 the Church of Sweden introduced so-called "confirmation classes" as a way of preparing young people for their first Holy Communion. There was a very strong incentive for the participants to pass the test. Those who were not admitted were not aloud to get married!

In 1806, *Anders* moved some ten kilometers south to the croft of Norra Timmervik, where he served as a farmhand to the soldier Per Silfverdahl, who was the successor of the Silfverdahl, who had been taken to Russia as a prisoner of war 18 years earlier.[37] In the next Hearing Register, *Anders* is till listed under Norra Timmervik, with the comment "frail, right hand lame".[38] In 1811 *Anders* moved to the large homestead of Balltorp, which was located just north of Simonstorp, where his family had its roots. At this time, he worked as a "dependent farm hand", which indicates that the parish subsidized his cost of living. The following year, a new maid was hired at the same farm. Her name was *Kerstin Olsdotter*, she was born in 1789, and a few years later she would become the wife of *Anders Olsson* and eventually the mother of *Cajsa Andersdotter*.[39]

Chapter 2:

Cajsa Andersdotter's maternal ancestors

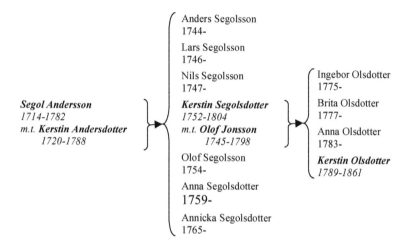

Hard labor, starvation and disease

Dalbergsån is the name of a creek which formed the border between the parishes of Bolstad and Grinstad. Shortly before the creek flows into Lake Vänern, even a strip of land north of the creek belonged to Bolstad Parish. This was the location of a manor named Kambol, which had a history dating back to the 16th century. In the middle of the 18th century, Kambol was a large estate of almost six hides[2] with another 13 hides of subordinate homesteads.[40] From 1737, the estate was owned by Colonel Abraham Segerfeldt. After his death in 1753, it was inherited by his daughter, the Countess Anna Margareta Cronhielm, who owned it until 1776, when it was purchased by Colonel Carl Jacob von Quanten. Two years later, he renamed the manor Quantensborg (later Qvantenburg) and declared it an entailed estate, which meant that it would be inherited, undivided, by the oldest son in each future generation of his family.

---

[2] Assessment unit of land.

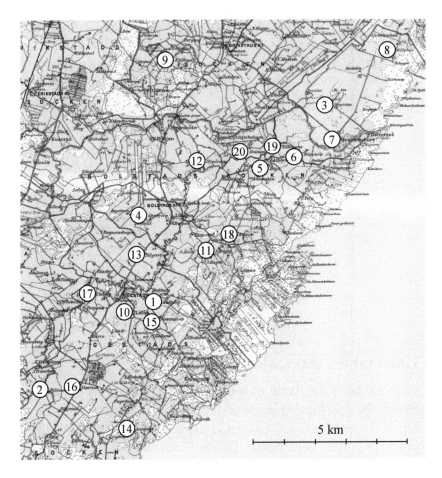

Parts of the parishes of Grinstad, Bolstad and Gestad.
Detail from map of Sundal Judicial District 1895.[41]

1. Balltorp
2. Björnerud
3. Bredgården
4. Glysbyn
5. Höga
6. Högstorp
7. Kambol/Qvantenburg

8. Kläven
9. Kövan
10. Löfås
11. Norra Åker
12. Nygården
13. Rågtvet
14. Sannebo

15. Simonstorp
16. Skerrud
17. Stora Uleberg
18. Södra Rödjan
19. Tillhagen
20. Övre Holmen

One of the subordinate homesteads of Kambol, and later Qvan-tenburg, was Övre Holmen, just south of Dalbergsån, which covered a land area of one hide. This is where we find the first trace of *Cajsa Andersdotter's* maternal ancestors. Since Övre Holmen was in possession of the noble family, who resided at Kambol, it was a so-called gentry homestead and, thus, exempt from taxes. Before 1789, noble families were not allowed to sell their land to commoners, but there was no law forbidding them to lease it. Such leased gentry land was known as "gentry taxed homesteads" since, as opposed to the noble family who owned the land, the tenant farmers were liable to pay taxes.

One of the tenants at Övre Holmen was *Segol Andersson* (1714-1782), who later would become the mother's mother's father of *Cajsa Andersdotter*. The first evidence of his presence at Övre Holmen dates back to 1744. At this time, he was 30 years old, and married to *Kerstin Andersdotter*, who was 24. They leased one fourth of the land of the homestead.[42] *Segol* and *Kerstin* remained at Övre Holmen for many years and had seven children, who all survived to adult age:[43]

- Anders, born in 1744
- Lars, born in 1746
- Nils, born in 1747
- *Kerstin*, born in 1752
- Olof, born in 1754
- Anna, born in 1759
- Annika, born in 1765

In the Tax Registers, which were renewed annually as a basis for the tax levy, one can find fairly detailed information about each household. The entries for *Segol Andersson's* family include the following facts:

1750 – *Segol* and his wife *Kerstin* are the only persons liable to pay taxes on their land of 1/4 homestead.[44]

1758 – Their son Anders turns 14 and is registered as an adult, liable to pay taxes.[45]

1760 – Anders moves to Södra Rödjan, where he starts to work as a farmhand. It was a general rule that children of small-holders left home to start working as soon as they had reached the age of 15. There were two obvious reasons for this. The harvest of the parent's portion of land was not sufficient to feed the entire household, and the family did not have the resources to pay taxes for grown children still residing at home.[46]

1761 – Anders returns from Södra Rödjan to work at his parents' farm. In contrast, Lars, their second son, now 15 years old, moves out to work as a farmhand, probably at the gentry estate Lövås in the parish of Gestad. At least he is said to return from there in 1765.[47]

1762 – Anders returns to Södra Rödjan. Nils, the third son of *Segol* and *Kerstin*, is now 15 years old, and as a result, considered liable to pay taxes.[48]

1764 – Nils moves to Glysbyn to work as a farmhand.[49]

1765 – Lars returns from Lövås.[50]

1766 – This year the household consists of eight people: *Segol, Kerstin,* their son Lars, three minors, and two elderly occupants. The minors must be *Kerstin*, Olof, and Anna. Obviously, the Tax Officer disregarded Annika, who was only one year old. Since Catechetical Hearing Registers did not exist in Bolstad until 1768, we cannot find the names of the two elderly residents. It seems probable that either *Segol's* or *Kerstin's* parents temporarily lived with the family.[51]

1767 – The two elderly residents of the household have moved.[52]

1768 – Lars still works on the farm, but only two minors remain. Apparently, the daughter *Kerstin*, now 16, has found work as a maid on some other farm.[53]

1769 – *Segol* extends his leased land area to 1/2 hide. The household now consists of him, his wife, their son Lars, but also their daughter Kerstin, who must have returned from her position as a maid. Only two minors remain at home, since the son Olof, now 15, like his older siblings has moved out to work for someone else.[54]

1770 – According to the first Catechetical Hearing Register of Bolstad 1768-74, the son Anders, along with his wife, Catharina, born in 1740, and their daughter, Britta, born in 1770, live with *Segol* and *Kerstin* at Övre Holmen.[55] The Tax Register states that one maid (= Catharina?) is added to the household. There is also a marginal note: "Son Anders at manor", which probably indicates that Anders lives with his parents, but works and pays taxes at the land owner's manor, Kambol.[56]

1771 – This year the family consists of *Segol* and *Kerstin*, their grown children Nils and *Kerstin*, and their two minor children Anna and Annika. Evidently, both Lars and his brother Anders with wife and child have moved away. On the other hand, Nils must have returned from his employment at another location.[57] This summer the crops fail, and during the following winter many impoverished Swedes suffer from famine.

1772 – Although *Segol* is only 58 years old, he transfers the responsibility for his leased farm to his 18-year-old son Olof, who has just returned home. Thus, *Segol* and *Kerstin* become dependent tenants of their own son.[58] Have they surrendered to crop failure and starvation, or do they pass the farm over to their son to reduce the tax levy, since dependent tenants were not liable to pay taxes? This year, the crops turn out even worse than the preceding year, and many stories still remain describing how poverty-stricken Swedes were forced to dilute their bread with bark, lichen and straw to survive. In the parishes of Bolstad, Gestad and Grinstad, 293 people die, a substantial increase compared to normal years. In 121 of these cases, the cause of death is stated as dysentery, an infection of the intestines, often caused by malnourishment and exposure to contaminated food or water.

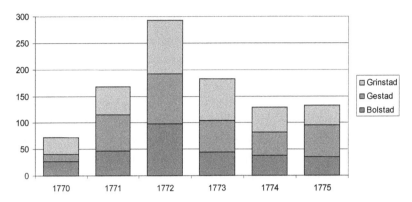

Number of deaths in Bolstad, Gestad, and Grinstad 1770-75.[59]

*During the years 1772 and 1773 more people died of famine and disease than was ever registered during the 170 years that have passed since the Census in Sweden was established – more victims than wars, the 1809 militia epidemic (= dys*entery and typhoid fever) *or cholera ever harvested.*[60]

It is worth noting that 1772 was the year when King Gustav III performed a coup, taking over power from Parliament. This change of power marked the end of the so-called Age of Liberty and soon led to new wars.

1773 – Tax Register missing.

1774 – The land of Övre Holmen is no longer leased to tenant farmers. Instead, it is noted as "farmed under Kambol". Perhaps the tenants were unable to pay their rent because of failing crops and, as a result, were evicted. However, they seem to remain in the village, because their names are still listed in the Tax Register, but they are not considered liable to pay taxes. Most probably, they simply owned nothing that could be taxed.[61] *Segol's* and *Kerstin's* daughter *Kerstin*, who has now turned 21, decides to move ten kilometers south to a farm called Björnerud no. 6 in the parish of Gestad, where she will work as a maid.

1775 – One of the earlier tenants at Övre Holmen returns to farm 1/2 hide. A new tenant farms 1/4 hide. The last 1/4 hide continues to be farmed under Kambol. *Segol* and his wife still live in the village with their two remaining, minor children, but they do not lease any ground and are registered as impoverished.[62]

1776 – Colonel von Quanten acquires Kambol, including all underlying homesteads. *Segol's* and *Kerstin's* son Olof returns as tenant of the last 1/4 hide of Övre Holmen. His parents live with him and are classified as "elderly". *Segol's* and *Kerstin's* daughter Anna, now seventeen years old, has moved away from home.[63]

1777 – The daughter Anna returns home and takes over the lease from her brother Olof, who moves to Högstorp to work as a farmhand. *Segol* and *Kerstin* are again described as "elderly".[64]

The farmhand who almost took over the farm

At this point, we temporarily leave the development at Övre Holmen to focus on what happened at the farm Björnerud no. 6 in Gestad Parish, to which *Segol's* and *Kerstin's* daughter *Kerstin* moved in 1774. Björnerud was a taxed homestead, which means that the farmers owned the land themselves and paid taxes to the state. Together, the land of the farms at Björnerud, added up to one hide. In 1773, a land surveyor came to initiate the so-called great redistribution. In the minutes from this meeting, Björnerud is described as:

> *This homestead is located on the flatland, owns enough land for grazing but very little forest, hardly enough for fence building and firewood. All fields consist of clay soil with no other discrepancy than that they have been differently fertilized. The fields are very flat and probably subject to flooding, since several of them have no drainage...*[65]

In 1761, the homestead Björnerud consisted of six farms. The land of farm no. 6 covered an area of 1/8 hide. The owner was a man named Anders Nilsson, born in 1732. His wife, Anna Elofs-

Map of Björnerud with surrounding infields at the great redistribution in 1773. Land belonging to Björnerud no. 6 is marked with the letter B.

dotter, was born in 1737. In 1764, Anna bore a son, named Nils, who would remain his parents' only child.[66] Farmhands and maids changed positions from year to year, but near the end of the 1760's, a farmhand by the name of *Olof Jonsson*, born in 1745, was employed. He remained on the farm for a number of years.[67]

On April 21, 1770, the master of the farm, Anders Nilsson, unexpectedly died of a disease.[68] The estate inventory performed after his death,[69] presents a detailed picture of the farm. The real property was valued at 400 riksdaler, and the personal property, including household equipment, clothes, and farm animals (one horse, three cows, one bull, one bull calf, four sheep, one ram, and two pigs), amounted to 192 riksdaler. The total assets of the decedent estate were thus valued at 592 riksdaler, while payable debts amounted to 150 riksdaler. From the estate inventory, we can conclude, that Anders Nilsson and Anna Elofsdotter had purchased the farm together. The inventory describes this transaction, stating that Anders "purchased one half with the birthright of his wife." This suggests that Anders had bought half of the estate using the emptive right of his wife as a relative of the previous owner. Anna had bought the other half with her "acquired property assets at Lövbråten," which apparently refers to a compensation she had received for her inherited share of her parents' farm at Lövbråten in the parish of Frändefors. Presumably, one of her brothers had traded money for her inherited share of the land, in order to farm the entire estate by himself.

According to the National Law of 1734, the partition of inherited property should be settled in the following three stages:

- In the first stage, the surviving spouse obtained his/her "favored article" from the estate. He/She had the right to make a free choice, but was restricted to personal property, and the value could not exceed 1/20 of the total value of the estate (Marriage Law, chapter 17, § 1). According to the estate inventory, Anna Elofdotter chose two riksdaler in silver coins as her favored article.

- In the second stage, a widow obtained her "morning gift", which was a portion of property that her husband had bequeathed to her at the time of their marriage. The value of the morning gift was not to exceed 1/10 of the value of the estate, and if it formed part of the real property, it must be returned to the husband's heirs upon the death or remarriage of the widow (Marriage Law, chapter 9, § 4). The estate inventory states that Anna Elofsdotter received a ram valued at two riksdaler as her morning gift. Thus, this must have been what her husband had promised her at their wedding.

- In the third and final stage, the surviving spouse obtained his/her "marital property" from the estate. In the countryside, it amounted to 2/3 of the value of the estate for widowers, and

1/3 for widows (Marriage Law, chapter 10, § 2). In the cities, it was 1/2 for both sexes. Subsequently, the children shared the remaining assets as their inheritance (Inheritance Law, chapter 2, § 3).

In this specific case, the estate inventory states that, after the widow had obtained her favored article and her morning gift, the remaining estate was divided into three equally valued shares. By drawing lots, Anna was bestowed one share as marital property, and Nils the remaining two as inheritance. From each share, personal property valued at 50 riksdaler was auctioned in order to pay the debts of the estate. In the auction sale, the farmhand *Olof Jonsson* gave winning bids for a blue vest, a green vest, a water bucket, an auger, and a drawbar with chain.

However, *Olof* was not content with taking over two of his former master's vests. On February 15, 1771, a little over a year after his master's death, he married the widow Anna Elofsdotter, despite the fact that she was eight years his senior.[70] In this way, *Olof* took over the management of the farm.[71] On February 28, the following year, Anna bore him a daughter, whom they named Kerstin.[72] However, their period of mutual happiness was brief. On April 25, Anna died from complications of child birth. On the same day, baby Kerstin died of an unknown childhood disease.[73] The son Nils, now eight years old, had thus lost both of his biological parents. All he had left was his stepfather *Olof*, the former farmhand of his parents' farm.

After Anna Elofsdotter's death, the farm Björnerud no. 6 faced another estate distribution. The divided property was limited to the possessions of Anna, which corresponded to 1/3 of the total value of the estate. The 2/3 of the estate that Nils had previously inherited from his father was not included. I have not found any estate inventory following the passing of Anna Elofsdotter, but according to the Inheritance Law, *Olof Jonsson* must have obtained 2/3 of her belongings as marital property, while the remaining assets must have been awarded to Nils as inheritance. However, the Marriage Law, chapter 10, § 2, stated that, land and buildings, which the deceased person had acquired <u>before</u>

the marriage, were not included in the marital property of the remaining spouse. Thus, *Olof's* marital property could only have been part of Anna's personal property, since she had acquired the farm together with her previous husband, Anders Nilsson, before she married *Olof*. All of her real property must have been awarded to Nils, but it is not clear whether *Olof* had sufficient legal knowledge to realize that this was the case. When a land surveyor arrived at Björnerud to perform the great redistribution on May 17, 1773, according to the minutes of the meeting, *Olof* either ignorantly or falsely introduced himself as "part owner of the farm and stepfather of the minor Nils". However, an appointed custodian of Nils was also present at the meeting to monitor his interests. His name was Eric Larsson, from Lövbråten, the homestead of Nils' biological mother's family.[74]

From this point on, *Olof* took full responsibility for the farm and his stepson, Nils. It must have been difficult for one person to manage the chores in the fields and simultaneously run a household. Understandably, *Olof* decided to hire a maid. At the start of the working year, the last week of September, in 1773, the maid arrived at the farm. She is already familiar to the reader: *Kerstin Segolsdotter*, twenty-one years of age, from Övre Holmen in Bolstad Parish. *Kerstin* must have been a valued maid, because *Olof* soon asked her to marry him. As they are not recorded in Bolstad Marriage Register, we do not know the exact date of their wedding, but it must have happened no later than 1774. According to the Tax Register of this year, the household consisted of one husband (*Olof*), one wife (*Kerstin*) and one child (their stepson Nils).[75] In the Catechetical Hearing Register of 1768-74, the word "married" is noted for *Kerstin* and the name of Anna Elofsdotter as the wife of *Olof* is crossed out and replaced by *Kerstin's*.[76] In the following Catechetical Hearing Register, which was begun in 1775, *Olof* and *Kerstin* are noted as the residents of Björnerud no. 6 and as the parents of the stepson Nils.[77] On November 16, 1775, *Kerstin* gave birth to their first child, a daughter by the name of Ingebor.[78] At this point, the life of *Olof* and *Kerstin* took a new course. In 1776, they left Björnerud to move just over four kilometers southeast to Sanne-

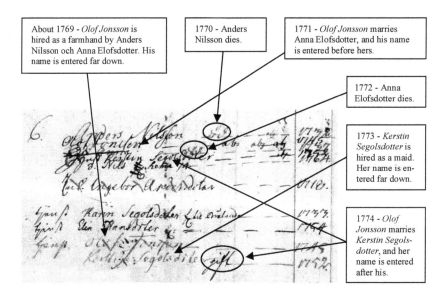

About 1769 - *Olof Jonsson* is hired as a farmhand by Anders Nilsson och Anna Elofsdotter. His name is entered far down.

1770 - Anders Nilsson dies.

1771 - *Olof Jonsson* marries Anna Elofsdotter, and his name is entered before hers.

1772 - Anna Elofsdotter dies.

1773 - *Kerstin Segolsdotter* is hired as a maid. Her name is entered far down.

1774 - *Olof Jonsson* marries Kerstin Segolsdotter, and her name is entered after his.

Detail from Gestad Catechetical Hearing Register 1768-74.[79]
The Swedish words "död" = dead, and "gift" = married.

bo on the shore of Lake Vänern.[80] Perhaps a conflict with Nils' custodian was the motivation for their move, since Nils did not accompany them. Instead, he probably moved to his mother's relatives in Lövbråten, while Björnerud no. 6 was leased out.[81] Through the minutes of a meeting held between the land surveyor and the farmers, concerning a border conflict between Björnerud and the neighboring homesteads, we know, with certainty, that the farm was not sold. The meeting was held on August 20, 1784, and Nils is listed as the owner of the farm. [82] The legal age of majority in 18th century Sweden was twenty-one years, so although Nils was twenty, he was still represented by a custodian. The custodian was Eric Elofsson of Lövbråten, which we can assume is Nils's maternal uncle.

During their time in Sannebo, *Olof Jonsson* and *Kerstin Segolsdotter* had a second daughter, Britta, born in 1777.[83] She was, however, not entered in the Gestad Birth and Baptism Register. A year later, they moved to *Kerstin's* childhood home at Övre Holmen in the parish of Bolstad, where they were hired as servants.[84]

Back to square one

For practical reasons, it has been difficult to trace all the seven children of *Segol Andersson* and *Kerstin Andersdotter* as they move between farms in the area, working as farmhands or maids, until they eventually marry and find more permanent homesteads. Therefore, I have decided to focus on the events that occur at the parents' home, Övre Holmen, and at the fate of the daughter *Kerstin Segolsdotter*. After all, she is the one who later became the grandmother of *Cajsa Andersdotter*. Now, however, as we return to Övre Holmen, *Kerstin's* brothers and sisters will again form part of the story.

As you may remember, in 1777, *Kerstin's* sister Anna had taken over the lease of their parents' 1/4 hide farm from her brother Olof, who had moved to Högstorp to work as a farmhand. At the same time, Anna had taken over the responsibility of their aging parents, *Segol* and *Kerstin,* who still lived as dependent tenants at the farm. Again, the Tax Registers describe what happened year by year.

1779 – Olof Segolsson takes back the lease from his sister Anna, and extends the area to 1/2 hide. Secondarily, the Tax Register confirms that *Olof Jonsson, Kerstin Segolsdotter*, and their two daughters, Ingebor and Britta, have become residents at Övre Holmen, stating that the number of occupants, aside from the master, now includes one farmhand (*Olof Jonsson*), two maids (the sisters *Kerstin* and Anna), and two children (*Olof's* and *Kerstin's* daughters). [85]

1780 – Olof Segolsson marries a woman named Anna Larsdotter, born in 1758.[86] The wedding is not documented in Bolstad Marriage Register.

1781 – On August 13, *Kerstin Segolsdotter* gives birth to a third girl, who is named Anna.[87] Two month later, on October 26, her sister-in-law Anna Larsdotter gives birth to her first child, a daughter named Annika.[88]

1782 – On August 25, the oldest member of the family, *Segol Andersson*, dies from "throat sickness" (probably diphtheria) at the age of 68.[89] Three weeks later, on September 15, the youngest member of the family, Olof Segolsson's and Anna Larsdotter's daughter, Annika, dies of smallpox, before she has reached the age of one.[90] In all likelihood, *Olof Jonsson's* and *Kerstin Segolsdotter's* youngest daughter faces the same fate, because the word "dead" is written after her name in the Catechetical Hearing Register, although she is not entered into the Death and Funeral Register.

1783 – On August 25, Anna Larsdotter gives birth to a son, who is named Olof.[91] *Kerstin Segolsdotter* bears a daughter, who is given the name of her deceased, older sister, Anna. Her birth is not listed in the Bolstad Birth and Baptism Register.

1784 – *Olof Jonsson, Kerstin Segolsdotter*, and their three daughters move one kilometer southeast to a cottage in the neighboring village of Höga.[92]

Olof Segolsson remains another few years as a tenant farmer at Övre Holmen.[93] His siblings, who live in the surrounding villages, take turns assisting him with the farm. In 1787, Olof cancels the lease and moves away with his family, primarily to Bredgården in the parish of Grinstad[94] and later to Skerrud in the parish of Gestad.[95] At the same time, his mother *Kerstin Andersdotter* moves in with her youngest daughter Annika, who is now married and lives with her family at Klövan in Grinstad Parish. There, *Kerstin* passes away from pneumonia on May 1, 1788, at the age of 68.[96]

At this point, we leave Övre Holmen for good to focus on the continued story of *Kerstin Segolsdotter, Olof Jonsson* and their daughters. As previously mentioned, in 1784, they moved to a cottage at Höga, one kilometer southeast of Övre Holmen. In the minutes of a meeting from 1787, when the land surveyor initiated the great redistribution at Höga, *Olof* is not listed among the owners of land. Obviously, he had not purchased their cottage but leased it.[97] The inclusion of a single word in the Catechetical Hearing Register again emphasizes how the aggressive foreign policy of King Gustav III influenced the life of poor populations living in rural geographical areas. In 1773, Russia and Denmark had signed an agreement to support each other in the event of an outbreak of war. When Gustav III attacked Russia in 1788, the Russian Tsar demanded help from Denmark. The Danish king, reluctantly, sent an army from Norway into the Swedish provinces of Bohuslän, Värmland and Dalsland. Since the Swedish armed forces were sent to invade Saint Petersburg, the Danish-Norwegian forces met very little resistance. In the beginning of October, they occupied the cities of Uddevalla, Vänersborg and Åmål. Local militia units were hastily established, but there was an insufficient amount of time to train the newly recruited soldiers. In the Catechetical Hearing Register of Bolstad 1787-96, the word "lantvärn" (= local militia) after *Olof Jonsson's* name, indicates that he was part of such a unit.[98] While the Danish-Norwegian army advanced towards Gothenburg, Gustav III, with the diplomatic support of England and Prussia, succeeded in negotiating an armistice and later established peace with Denmark. The Danish losses in this so-called "show war" amounted to five persons killed in battle but more than one thousand victims of starvation and disease.

On August 1, 1789, a fourth and last daughter was born to *Olof* and *Kerstin*. She was named *Kerstin* after her mother.[99] Apparently, the resources of the family were insufficient for both paying taxes and feeding everyone. As soon as the three older daughters turned fourteen, they therefore left home to start working as maids. At this point, several dramatic changes occurred in the life of the family. On March 25, 1798, the father, *Olof*, died of dysentery.[100] Daughter number three, Anna, now moved back to Höga to help her mother and nine-year-old sister, *Kerstin*.[101] The following year, the oldest daughter, Ingebor, also returned home, but before she could be summoned to a Catechetical Hearing, she died suddenly of an unknown disease.[102] A few years later, in 1803, Anna, together with her mother, moved a few kilometers north to Tillhagen, a homestead under Qvantenburg, where they were both registered as domestic servants.[103] At about the same time, the daughter Brita met a farmhand called Pär Eriksson at the farm Kläven in the parish of Grinstad.[104] They married[105] and moved to Rågtvet in the parish of Gestad.[106] There, they received the girls' mother *Kerstin* as their dependent tenant, but she lived with them only for a short time, before she died from a fever on September 23, 1804.[107] Now, out of the original family of *Olof Jonsson* and *Kerstin Segolsdotter*, only the three youngest daughters remained: Brita, who had started a family, and Anna and *Kerstin,* who supported themselves working as maids at different farms in the area.

Complete estate inventories exist after both *Olof* and *Kerstin* (see supplements). They indicate that the material standard of the family was humble but not impoverished. As a tenant, *Olof* did not own any real property, but at his death he left a number of personal belongings behind: tools, household ware, clothing, a few farm animals (one sheep and two pigs), and some straw and hay. After debts were subtracted, the value of the decedent estate was estimated to about seven riksdaler. One surprising entry in his inventory is the following: "The widow's clothes were examined and evaluated to one riksdaler". Obviously, the widow's clothes were not considered her private property but part of her husband's estate. In the detailed estate inventory concerning Anders Nilsson of Björnerud, where *Olof,* in his twenties, had worked as a farmhand, the widow's clothes are not mentioned. Could it be that the registrars, who performed the inventories, had different opinions about what should be included in a decedent estate? Because *Olof* and *Kerstin* owned a sheep, a pair of sheep shears, a pair of carding combs, a spinning wheel, and a loom, it is fairly safe to assume that they made some of their clothing themselves. The decedent estate after *Kerstin,* however, also includes clothing made from silk, cotton, and calico (= cotton with printed patterns), so obviously some fabric must have been purchased. Strangely enough, no shoes are mentioned in the otherwise comprehensive inventories. Were the shoes so simple, that they had no financial value? Perhaps they were handmade? Among the objects listed in *Olof's* inventory is a "hide switch", a tool made of wood switches for softening dried hides. *Kerstin's* inventory includes a shoemaker's toolbox.

After *Olof's* death, according to the National Law of 1734, his widow *Kerstin* must have received her favored article, her morning gift and her marital property (= 1/3 of the value of the estate), before her daughters shared the rest as the inheritance. The value of the widow's portion must have been slightly less than four riksdaler. Six years later, when *Kerstin* passed away, the value of her estate was estimated to be almost seven riksdaler. Despite the fact that she was poor, she had obviously not spent any portion of her inherited money. On the contrary, she had increased her assets by a few riksdaler. At one point, she lent four riksdaler to a man called Anders Månsson at Holmen and then gained more than one riksdaler in interest. The loan and repaid interest confirms that *Kerstin* successfully managed her inheritance.

From what we have seen so far, it is obvious that entries are missing in Birth and Baptism Registers, Marriage Registers and Death and Funeral Registers from the 18th century in both Bolstad and Gestad. Another obvious fact is the imprecise age of deceased persons in the Death and Funeral Registers. For example, *Olof Jonsson's* age, in the Death and Funeral Register, is noted as 46 years, whereas the correct age according to the Catechetical Hearing Register should be 53. Were *Olof's* widow and children unaware of his exact age when the pastor asked? Or did the pastor make his own estimate, based on the physical appearance of the body of the deceased? After all, it must have been easy to simply look up the birth year of a dead person in the Catechetical Hearing Register and calculate the correct age.

The maid with the illegitimate child

We now leave *Olof Jonsson's* and *Kerstin Segolsdotter's* two older daughters in order to concentrate on the future fate of their youngest, *Kerstin Olsdotter*. Like many other young maids and farmhands in those days, she moved from employer to employer nearly every year. Several factors can explain the frequent employment changes of young people during this time.

– They may have had an ambition to qualify themselves for better employment options by widening their experience.

– They might have been searching for a partner in marriage, hoping to find someone suitable at their next place of work.

– They may have felt uncomfortable with their present employer and wanted to try their luck working for someone else.

The employment of farmhands and maids was regulated by the Employment Act of 1664. It stated that parents had the right to retain their children at home, to be engaged in work, until they turned 21. Then, children were free to apply for work elsewhere. Employment contracts were signed for a term of one year. A resignation notice had to be given between mid-July and mid-August, and the move to a new employer occurred during the last week of September, which in 1833, was changed to the last week of October. When a farmhand or maid resigned, the master was required to write a certificate with comments about the servant. This certificate was presented to the new employer, who in turn wrote an employment contract and made an advance salary payment.

Servants were not allowed to resign from their position during the contract year, and the Employment Act suggested different measures to make it difficult for discontented farmhands and maids to run away. They were required to leave the chest containing their personal belongings with the employer, who in turn had the right to capture runaway servants and bring them back by force. On the other hand, employers were not allowed to dismiss employees during the contract year, unless they had a legal reason, such as considering the servant to be "negligent, refractory, disorderly without accepting reprimands, disloyal, or else incompetent for their duty." Furthermore, it was illegal for able-bodied persons to be unemployed or "defenseless," which was the term for laborers willfully abstaining from work. In such cases, the Sheriff could intervene, and the person could be sentenced to penal labor.

The Employment Act further regulated the rights and duties of employers and employees. For example, employees had the right to room and board, a salary, and certain care in case of sickness or injury, and he had the right to complain to the Senior Enforcement Officer or the Sheriff if the employer did not fulfill his responsibilities. Those who had worked for thirty years or more for the same employer had the right to remain with him and enjoy room and board as a benefit for the remainder of their lives. The employer, on the other hand, had the right to corporally punish employees who failed to fulfill their duties. In 1858, this right was modified so that it would only apply to boys under the age of eighteen and girls under the age of sixteen.

In 1803 *Kerstin Olsdotter* was employed for the first time. She was then 14 years old, and her parental home in Högatorp no longer existed. Her father had passed away five years earlier, and her mother and older sister had moved out. *Kerstin* first served in Jöns Hammarström's household at the soldier's croft of Norra Åker, in Bolstad Parish.[108] After one year, she moved one kilometer west to the farm of Pär Eriksson at Rågtvet no. 2 in Gestad Parish.[109] The following year, she transferred to Nygården, which was located in the northern part of Bolstad Parish, between the two creeks Lillån and Dalbergsån, immediately west of Övre Hagen, the childhood home of her mother. Evidently, *Kerstin* liked this place, because she remained there for four years. In 1809, she decided to move back to Rågtvet. At least this must have been what she told the pastor, according to a note in the Catechetical Hearing Register.[110] However, *Kerstin* did not reappear at Rågtvet, which creates some uncertainty.

In this book, the reader follows *Kerstin Olsdotter's* fate from childhood to old age. In order to gather data for the story, for natural reasons, I worked my way in the opposite direction. I followed her backwards in time, from year to year, and from register to register. I lost track of her in the Catechetical Hearing Register of Gestad 1809-13, where she is listed as a maid in the household of Sven Jonsson at Balltorp no. 4, without information about her previous location.[111] Is she really identical to the *Kerstin Olsdotter* who left Nygården in Bolstad in 1809 with the intention to move to Rågtvet, not to Balltorp which is located two kilometers further south? We can be fairly certain that this is the case since both name (Kerstin Olsdotter), year of birth (1789) and place of birth (Bolstad) coincide.[112] According to the not quite complete Birth and Baptism Register, only one person by that name was born in Bolstad that year. Furthermore, there is an explanation to why *Kerstin* could not carry out the move as she had planned.

In 1764, at the time of the great redistribution, the homestead Rågtvet was divided between six independent farmers who lived in a central village.[113] In 1805, the number of land owners had increased to eight.[114] The following year, Christer G. Zelow, Lieutenant-Colonel and Marshal of the Court, purchased the estate Lövås in Gestad Parish. At the same time, he acquired the complete homestead of Rågtvet. According to the Tax Register of 1806, nineteen families, both farmers and employees, were forced to leave the land. For most of them, no destination is specified. In the margin of the register, there is a note stating that Rågtvet is now "farmed under Lövås".[115] Almost certainly, Christer Zelow's motif for acquiring Rågtvet was his interest in innovative farming. He needed more land to develop his ideas. In 1815, he designed a new barn intended to "house 110 cattle of both sexes, roaming loosely in 16 secluded departments."[116] On the map from a redistribution of land in 1827, the whole village of Rågtvet is replaced by a single, large, U-shaped construction, which corresponds to Zelow's drawing. According to the minutes of meeting, there is only one owner of the lands, Zelow himself.[117] It hardly comes as a surprise that Kerstin Olsdotter could not return as a maid to Rågtvet in 1809, considering that

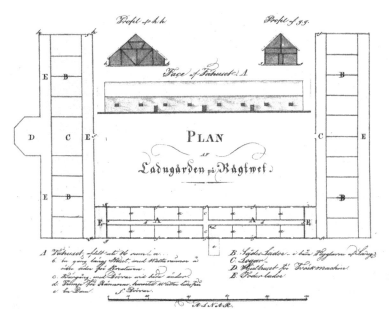

Christer G. Zelow's drawing of the new barn at Rågtvet.

there were no farmers living there anymore. Neither is she to be found among the servants of Zelow in Lövås. In all likelihood she was at the last moment offered a position as a maid at Balltorp instead. *Kerstin* was 20 years old when she started to work at Balltorp in 1809. Two years later, she resigned to apply for a position in the household of Lars Olsson at Stora Uleberg no. 2.[118] There, she would be the only maid for a young family who had recently had their first child. This would probably be considered as a valuable future qualification, since she would be responsible for all different tasks in the household. *Kerstin* must have moved to her new employer during the last week of September, but she quickly encountered unforeseen problems. According to the Catechetical Hearing Register, the mistress of the house was "over two years almost continuously bed-ridden with gout," but to make matters even worse, within a few months in her new position, *Kerstin* discovered that she herself was expecting a baby! In this situation, she returned to Balltorp, where she almost certainly had friends, and where there were more maids to share the burdens of work. We do not know if she ran away from her master Lars Olsson, or if he took action, founded on the legal grounds of his employer rights, to dissolve the employment contract. In any case, according to the Employment Act, *Kerstin* must have lost her right to obtain her salary and was possibly even subject to fines. On May 4, 1812, she bore an illegitimate child, a girl named Maja Stina.[119] In the Catechetical Hearing Register, after *Kerstin's* name, there is a note: "Impoverished, cannot support herself and the child".[120]

Kerstin's fate raises many questions. She must have become pregnant in late August of 1811. At that time, she had already resigned from Balltorp. In all probability, she did not know that she was pregnant when she moved to Stora Uleberg a month later, or she would not have taken on the demanding task that awaited her there. And who was the father of her child? In the Birth and Baptism Register we find a note: "The father is said to be the farmhand Anders Jonsson of the same household", but the pastor must have misheard, because there was no farmhand named Anders Jonsson at Balltorp, neither in 1811 nor in 1812. What *Kerstin* had mumbled, looking down at the floor, was most probably the name of the man, who is listed directly before her in the Catechetical Hearing Register, the dependent farmhand *Anders Olsson*, born in 1778, described as "frail, right hand lame".

As we already know, *Anders* had moved to Balltorp in 1811, as regulated by the Employment Act in the last week of September, which must have been the same week that *Kerstin* moved away from there. In all likelihood, they already knew each other, since Gestad was no large parish. At the very least, they must have seen each other in church on Sundays during the previous year, since attendance at the Sunday service was mandatory. Could it be that *Kerstin* was the reason that *Anders*, after five years in Norra Timmervik, resigned his employment there in order to move to Balltorp? But if this was the case, why did *Kerstin* move away? Could it be that she wanted to qualify herself to be able to contribute more, financially, to support a family where the husband was disabled? And if *Anders* was the father of Maja

Stina, why did he not marry *Kerstin* to spare her the shame of bearing an illegitimate child? The answer to the last question is simple. According to a note in the Catechetical Hearing Register, *Kerstin* was not yet admitted to Holy Communion and thus, according to the rules of the Church, not eligible to get married!

Even though the Church prevented *Anders* and *Kerstin* from getting married, they continued to live together as husband and wife. In the Catechetical Hearing Register of 1814-18 they are listed as dependent tenants at Balltorp and are described as impoverished.[121] On May 2, 1815, *Kerstin* bears their second daughter, Inga,[122] but in February the following year, the baby passes away without any mention of the cause of death.[123] Now, finally, something positive happens. *Kerstin*, at the age of 27, is admitted to Holy Communion. As a result, the rules of the Church can no longer prevent *Anders* from marrying her. On July 7, 1816, they have the banns published, and on Saturday, August 10, of the same year, they celebrate their wedding.[124] Now they no longer have to endure the humiliation of living together without being married, and though they are still impoverished, they are assigned a home of their own: a hill cottage at Hagen under Simonstorp.[125]

Chapter 3:

Cajsa Andersdotter's childhood and youth

Anders Olsson Landgren
1778-1853
m.t. **Kerstin Olsdotter**
1789-1861

Maja Stina Andersdotter
1812-1842
Greta Cajsa Andersdotter
1818-1907
Johannes Andersson
1829-

"So terrible I'd rather forget it"

The new home of *Anders Olsson, Kerstin Olsdotter*, and their four-year-old daughter Maja Stina, was a hill cottage. It was dug into the side of a hill and had walls, partly built of logs, partly consisting of the soil of the hill. Stamped earth formed the floor. Most probably, there was only one room in the cottage, with an open hearth for cooking, benches fixed to the walls for sleeping and sitting, and a table for eating and working. It is easy to imagine how drafty and cold it must have been in winter, when the open hearth was the only source of heat.

Restored hill cottage from the first half of the 19th century.[126]

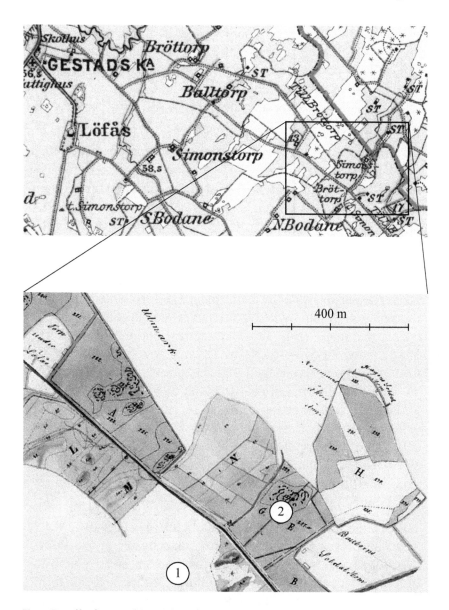

Top: Detail of map of Sundal Judicial District 1895.

Bottom: Combination of maps from the land redistributions of Balltorp in 1831 and Simonstorp in 1834. The section marked N belonged to Simonstorp. Those marked G and E belonged to Balltorp. Hans Ersson owned area E.

(1) = Hagen under Bröttorp.

(2) = Probable location of the hill cottage Hagen under Balltorp.

Adjacent to a hill cottage there was generally a small section of land, where the hill cottage dwellers, as their inhabitants were called, grew potatoes and kept some hens and maybe even a pig. The dwellers paid their rent in labor, which meant that they must serve the landlord a certain number of work days per year without being paid.

It is not quite easy to determine the exact location of the hill cottage of Anders and Kerstin, but by combining data from several sources, we can make a fairly safe assumption. Today, there is still a house called Hagen, but it is located on ground that belonged to the homestead of Bröttorp, while the hill cottage Hagen, according to the Catechetical Hearing Register of Gestad 1824-29 was located "in the hill between Simonstorp and Balltorp".[127] Initially, it was listed under Simonstorp, but around 1830, the pastor began to list it under Balltorp, where it was said to reside on ground owned by a man called Hans Ersson.[128] Analyzing the maps from the legal redistributions of Balltorp in 1831[129] and of Simonstorp in 1834,[130] we find a hill, not far from the present day Hagen under Bröttorp, which is located on the land of Balltorp, but near the land of Simonstorp. According to the minutes of meeting from the redistribution, half of the hill belonged to Hans Ersson. Thus, this location corresponds to all data found in the registers. Today, more than 180 years later, the sides of the hill are covered with forest, but on the south slope you can still see a recess in the side of the hill, which could well be the remains of the hill cottage.

The decline that *Anders'* family had experienced was bitter. His grandfather was a well-to-do farmer and owner of the farm Simonstorp no. 1, which formed 1/4 of the homestead Simonstorp. In the next generation, his six children had to sell the farm to share the inheritance. The oldest son leased the farm from the new owner, while his siblings had to find work as farmhands and maids, all except *Anders'* father who chose to become a reserve soldier. However, he disappeared when Anders was still a child, possibly killed in the war that Gustaf III launched against Russia in 1788. Now, *Anders* lived as an impoverished hill cottage

dweller, under the same homestead that his grandfather had partially owned fifty years earlier. This type of decline was not
unique. On the contrary, it was quite typical. From the end of the
18th century, Sweden's population grew rapidly, and the increase
became even more profound in the 19th century. A farm large
enough to sustain a family in the mid 18th century, could not
possibly feed a hundred great-grandchildren and their families
one hundred years later. This led to widespread poverty with
periods of starvation among the rural population. Many young
people were forced to move to the cities in an attempt to find
work in the growing industries. Others migrated to America,
hoping to improve their situation there.

Three explanations are usually mentioned when discussing the
rapid population growth:

Peace – During the 17th and 18th centuries, the kings of Sweden
fought repeated wars against neighboring countries. This devastated the country's economy and drained it of able-bodied men,
which caused serious problems for agricultural production. As a
result, the population suffered from starvation and hardship. The
last war against Denmark/Norway ended in 1814. Since then,
Swedes have lived in peace with improved living conditions.

Vaccine – The viral disease smallpox, with a mortality rate of
about 30 %, had plagued Europe and Asia for thousands of
years. At the end of the 18th century, the English doctor Edward
Jenner found that he could make children resistant to the virus
by intentionally infecting them with the milder disease cowpox.
The treatment was named vaccination after the Latin word vacca
= cow. In Sweden, the first vaccination was performed in 1801,
and by 1816 the government decided to make vaccination mandatory. In the 1830's, 80 % of all children were vaccinated, often
by the usher of the parish or by the school teacher. Nowadays,
smallpox is generally regarded as extinct in the whole world.

Potatoes – Towards the end of the 17th century, potatoes were
introduced as a new crop in Sweden. Later, when it was known
that the new vegetable could not only serve as food, but also as a

raw material for producing alcohol, it gained in popularity. The number of Swedes who grew potatoes increased rapidly, and since potatoes flourished in the Swedish climate and were rich in both vitamins and energy, the result was a decline in crop failure and famine.

The family of *Anders* and *Kerstin* is an excellent example of the importance of the vaccine. From the Death and Funeral Registers we can conclude that epidemics of smallpox raged in Gestad in 1768/69, 1781/82, 1788/89, and 1795/96. Between those peaks, only single cases occurred. From 1763 to 1811, the total number of dead in Gestad due to smallpox was 124. Almost all of the victims were children, which has a natural explanation. Since epidemics occurred regularly, more or less all children were exposed and infected. As a result, those who survived and lived to adult age were resistant to the virus. In the Catechetical Hearing Register of 1814-18, for the first time, there is a column stating which of the parishioners were resistant to smallpox. Both *Anders* and *Kerstin* are registered as "infected". It is possible that the pastor did not even have to ask before making the note in the register, since smallpox left very visible scars on the face and over the rest of the body. Maja Stina, on the contrary, could keep her skin smooth. Her note reads "vaccinated 1816". She and her siblings belonged to the first generation that would not have to endure this terrible sickness. [131] By the way, it was not only vaccination against smallpox that gave the children of the early 19th century better chances in life than their parents. As we have already mentioned, in 1811, the Church introduced regular confirmation courses to prepare young people for their first Holy Communion. As a result, Maja Stina was admitted to Communion when she was 14, as opposed to her parents who reached this point when they were 25 or 30. Thus, the rules of the Church no longer stopped parishioners from getting married once they had found a suitable partner.

After *Anders* and *Kerstin* moved to the hill cottage, six more children were born:

- Olle, born on July 13, 1817,[132] dead from stomach disease on July 29, the same year,[133]
- *Greta Cajsa*, born on June 30, 1818,[134]
- Lisa, born on January 17, 1821,[135] dead from dropsy on August 1, 1824,[136]
- Olof, born in 1823,[137] dead from chest pain on January 28, 1829,[138]
- Lisa, born on October 13, 1826,[139] dead in chest pain on February 24, 1828,[140] and
- Johannes, born on June 13, 1829.[141]

Thus, only three of *Anders'* and *Kerstin's* eight children reached adulthood.

It must have been difficult for the family to produce enough food for themselves and, at the same time, pay the rent for their hill cottage in days of work, considering the fact that Anders had only one good arm and Kerstin was almost continuously pregnant or nursing. According to the registers, they were impoverished, which means that they were exempt from paying taxes. They were also said to be paupers and, thus, received some subsidies from the parish.[142] The children were of little help. Maja Stina was the first one old enough to help with everyday work, but in her early teens she broke her right arm. Since poor people could not afford to see a doctor, it took years before her arm healed. When she was 17 and left home to work as a maid in the western neighbor parish Brålanda, she still had a "fragile right arm".[143] About 60 years later, her younger sister, *Greta Cajsa*, told her grand daughter *Elin Svensson* about her life, but all she would say about her childhood was that it was so poor and terrible that she would rather forget it.

Greta Cajsa was the next child in the family to reach adulthood. Like her sister, she remained at home until she had turned 17. Then she requested a relocation certificate to move to Brålanda, where she had found employment as a maid. In the Relocation Register her name has been mistaken for Greta Lisa, but there is

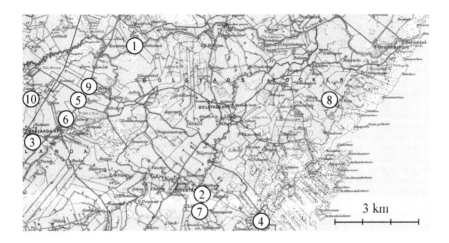

Parts of the parishes of Brålanda, Bolstad, and Gestad.
Detail from map of Sundal Judicial District 1895.[144]

1. Backerud	3. Brålanda	5. Hede	7. Simonstorp	9. Vena
2. Balltorp	4. Hagen	6. Noltorp	8. Södra Torp	10. Östebyn

no doubt about her identity, since all other details coincide. Before handing over the certificate, the pastor tested her reading ability, and awarded her the grade "fair", which was the best one given.[145] In Brålanda she worked one year at a farm called Noltorp and then at a tavern in Österbyn, which was a stop for coaches along the road from Åmål to Vänersborg. After two years in Brålanda, she returned to her parents in Hagen.[146] In the following Catechetical Hearing she probably protested against the name Lisa, and in the register the pastor has only written the name Greta. Her mother is now said to be sickly, and after her father's name there is a note: "Calls himself Landgren, has a lame right hand", and the name Landgren is added after Olsson.[147] At the end of this book, I will discuss the possible origin of the name Landgren.

Just like *Greta Cajsa,* her older sister Maja Stina moved back from Brålanda to Gestad in 1837. There she worked as a maid in Anders Andersson's household at Simonstorp no. 2, before moving back to her childhood home in Hagen to help her parents and her little brother Johannes, who was now nine years old. At the same time, *Greta Cajsa* moved out to serve first with Nils Andersson at Hede in Bolstad Parish [148] and later, in 1839, with C N A Hård and his wife Sara Eleonora Sevon in Vena.[149] When her employers moved to Backerud in 1840, she initially accompanied them there,[150] but soon returned to Nils Andersson at Hede. Here the name Greta is added later, and in all later registers she is only called *Cajsa*.[151] During 1839-40, Maja Stina also served as a maid at different farms, one of them being Södra Torp in Bolstad Parish.[152]

The homesteads of Hede, Vena and Backerud, where *Cajsa* worked, were located in the western part of Bolstad Parish, whereas Södra Torp where Maja Stina served was located in the eastern part. The distance between these areas is about eight kilometers, but half way between them, Bolstad church formed a natural meeting point. Here, the sisters must have met on Sundays. Was it while they were chatting together after the service that the idea occurred that they should apply for work together at some large estate further away from home? Perhaps a so-called commission agent or travelling employment officer made them an attractive offer? At any rate, the sisters decided to move to the manor of Onsjö outside Vänersborg.

On Wednesday, October 13, 1841, the sisters appear at the Parish Office to request their Relocation Certificates. Maja Stina, who is the oldest, presents her intentions first. She is to move to the farm Gäddebäck under Onsjö, located in the parish of Västra Tunhem on the eastern side of the river Göta Älv. When she has received her certificate, it is *Cajsa's* turn. She has been promised a position at the very manor Onsjö, which is located on the western side of the river in the parish of Vassända-Naglum, sometimes called Gustava in the Church Registers.[153] For *Cajsa*, the year at Onsjö would prove to be a high point in her life, which she loved to talk about in her old age. For her sister Maja Stina, it resulted in a catastrophe. On June 15, the following year, she returned to her parents "without certificate", which most probably means that she had fled. On July 3, she bore a stillborn, illegitimate male child, and on July 19 she died from complications of childbirth.[154]

They say that history repeats itself. Just like her mother *Kerstin Olsdotter*, 30 years earlier, Maja Stina must have become pregnant shortly before taking up her new post. Just like her mother, she was forced to leave her employer, breaking the rules of the Employment Act. This however, is where the similarities end. For *Kerstin Olsdotter*, the unplanned child became the beginning of a family. For Maja Stina it was the end of her life.

Onsjö Manor

The manor of Onsjö was located on the western side of the river Göta Älv and was one of the largest estates in what is today the municipality of Vänersborg. Next to the manor passed the road from the town of Vänersborg and on to the Parish of Västra Tunhem on the eastern side of the river. There was no bridge, so roadmen had to cross the river by ferry. The list of owners of the manor dates back to the 14th century and contains names from famous aristocratic families such as Oxenstierna, Natt och Dag, Soop, Frölich, and Leijonstolpe. In 1770, Colonel Wolrath Vilhelm Haij (1731-1803) purchased the estate. He had a new mansion built 1773-74 (see wash and photo), and in 1786 he declared Onsjö an entailed estate. His entailment declaration mandated that the eldest son in each generation would inherit the estate undivided, and that nothing – neither realty nor private property – could be sold or pawned. His intention was that the manor would remain the property of his family, and that his descendants would "by their personal rectitude honor the position they inherit from their parents" and, "given their opportunities and abilities, by faithful management of their earthly belongings, as far as possible, promote the perpetual existence of the family." [155] However, he assigned the widow of each holder of the entailed estate the right to remain in charge of the property until the end of her life. This probably led to a different development than he had intended. During a period of 54 years, following his death, women ruled the estate of Onsjö.

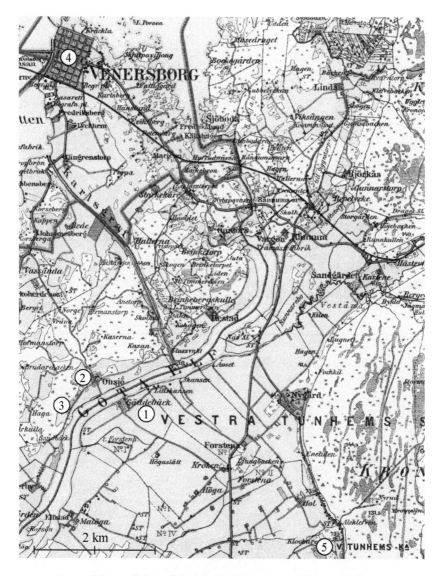

Parts of the parishes of Vassända-Naglums and Västra Tunhem.
Detail from map of Väne Judicial District 1895.[156]

1. Gäddebäck   3. Onsjö mortuary chapel   5. Västra Tunhem church
2. Onsjö estate   4. Vänersborg

Ferry across Göta Älv between Gäddebäck and Onsjö.
In the background, the main building of Onsjö Manor.
Wash by Gustaf Silfverstolpe 1806, Museum of Vänersborg.

Main building of Onsjö Manor. Photo from 1897, Museum of Vänersborg.

In addition to the manor itself, a number of surrounding home-steads and crofts were included in the entailed estate. The largest of these was Gäddebäck, on the eastern side of the river. Onsjö and Gäddebäck each covered the space of one hide, which indicated that they were large and important farms. Not far from the main building of Onsjö Manor, the founder had a mortuary chapel erected, where only the owners of the estate and their immediate families were to be sepulchered.

After the death of Wolrath Vilhelm Haij in 1803, his widow Catarina von Stockenström (1754-1827) claimed her right to succeed him as owner of the estate. Their son, Erik Henrik Wilhelm Haij (1773-1821), then chose to join the Swedish army in the so-called first Napoleonic war of 1805-07. To acknowledge his military achievements, he was awarded the highly noble, hereditary title of baron. However, he passed away before his mother, and never came into possession of Onsjö. After his mother's death, his widow, Charlotte Haij, born von Platen (1779-1860), the sister of the famous canal builder Baltzar von Platen, took command over the estate. As a result, their son Wolrath Wilhelm Haij (1804-1840), was unable to accede as owner of the estate. After having married Elisabeth Maria Söllscher (1804-1866) in 1827, Wolrath Wilhelm Haij decided to leave the estate and move to Vänersborg. It was not until after the death of Charlotte Haij in 1860, that a male successor came into possession of the estate. His name was Erik Wolrath Wilhelm Haij (1828-1903), and he was the great-grandson of the founder.

The entailed estate of Onsjö remained in the possession of the Haij family for over two hundred years. In 1963, Parliament passed a law stating that all entailed estates must be annulled at the death of the present possessor. The last owner of Onsjö as an entailed estate was thus Erik Wolrath Wilhelm Haij (1906-1973), great-great-great-grandson of the founder. He passed away without having produced any heirs. The municipality of Vänersborg then acquired the estate. At that time, the mansion was in a rather dilapidated state, and in 1982 it was finally destroyed due to arson.[157] Today, the surrounding grounds have been converted into a golf course.

A glass of water for the King

When *Cajsa Andersdotter* arrived at Onsjö the last week in October, 1841, the manor was ruled by the 62-year-old widow, Baroness Charlotte Haij, born von Platen. In the Catechetical Hearing Register,[158] we find a list of all the people residing at the manor. In addition to the baroness and her 27 year-old, unmarried daughter Nathalia, there were a number of servants: a house keeper, one foreman, two gardeners (one of whom with wife), a handmaid, five farmhands (one of whom with wife, son, and daughter), a shepherd boy, and four maids.

Cajsa Andersdotter, who refused to share any details about her impoverished childhood, loved to reminisce about the experience of her year at Onsjö. Having grown up in a one room, hillside cottage, where the naked earth formed the walls and floor, she must have been thoroughly overwhelmed when she entered the mansion, with its large halls, parquet flooring and walls covered with French hand painted wallpaper. In the Hearing Register she is listed among the maids, but according to what she later shared with her granddaughter, she was a chambermaid and wore a fine dress, with white gloves that extended to her elbows. Her main task at the mansion was to serve the gentry of the estate. She recounted that the King once came for a short visit. She appeared before the gentry and the other servants, to serve His Majesty a glass of water. As a tip, he bestowed upon her a whole riksdaler.[159] The credibility of *Cajsa's* story finds support in the following article from the local newspaper Wenersborgs Weckoblad, printed on Thursday, May 26, 1842.[160]

Snrifes Nyheter.

Wenersborg. H. K. H. Arfprinsen Hertig Oscar Fredrik af Östergötland, stadd på resan till Göteborg, för att derifrån åtfölja den expedition med Norrska Sjö-Kadet-ter, som innewarande år utgår, anlände hit i går förmiddag med ångfartyget Dan. Thunberg. H. K. H. befann sig i högönstlig wälmåga och emottog, under den korta tid ångfar-tyget här qwarlåg, uppwaktning af Länets Höfding med Che-ferne för Länsstyrelsens Departementer samt Chefen för West-göta-Dals Kongl. Regemente med de på befälsmöte härwa-rande Officerare jemte flere andre militäre och ciwile personer. Och täcktes H. K. H. äfwen göra en tour kring staden och bese densamma.

Translation to English:

Domestic news

Vänersborg. His Royal Highness, the Crown Prince Oscar Fredrik, Duke of Östergötland, on his way to Gothenburg, in order to join the expedition of Norwegian midshipmen, which will take place this present year, arrived here yes-terday morning on the steamship Daniel Thunberg.[161] *His Royal Highness was in a state of excellent well-being, and, during the short time the steamship remained here, was paid respects by the Governor, accompanied by the execu-tive leaders of the departments of the county's administra-tive board, and by the Colonel of Västgöta-Dal Regiment, together with the officers taking part in the local military meeting, as well as by numerous other military and civil-ian persons. It also pleased His Royal Highness to take a tour around the town to explore its points of interest.*

The fact that the deceased husband of the Baroness Charlotte Haij had participated in the military campaign against Napoleon as a Major-General and moved in the leading circles of the coun-try, makes it plausible that the Crown Prince during his "tour around the town" chose to visit Onsjö. When *Cajsa* recounted these events to her granddaughter *Elin* some sixty years later, it is quite natural that she called Oscar Fredrik "King" rather than

"Crown Prince". By then, he had ruled Sweden under the name of Oscar I from 1844 to 1859.

Crown Prince Oscar Fredrik
painted by Joseph Karl Stieler in 1821

The dead body in the bridal gown

Cajsa also told Elin that a daughter of the Haij family planned to marry, but the bridegroom failed to appear at the wedding. The bride, sick with sorrow and despair, slowly pined away. She was buried in the mortuary chapel of Onsjö, wrapped in her bridal gown.

As in the previous case, it has not been possible to verify the accuracy of this narrative, but it is unquestionably based on historical facts. The Baroness Charlotte Haij and her deceased husband, General Erik Henrik Wilhelm Haij, in addition to the daughter Nathalia, had another daughter named Lovisa Augusta, born in 1816. On May 3, 1835, the Cavalry Captain Gustaf Ehrensparre Ljungfelt, master of Dybeck Castle in Skåne, the southernmost province of Sweden, asked to have banns published to marry the 17 year younger Louise (= Lovisa) Haij, but the wedding never transpired.[162] Unfortunately, in the Banns and Marriage Register, the pastor failed to make a note to explain the last minute cancellation of the wedding. Three years later, Lovisa Augusta died on a trip to Linköping, shortly before her 22nd birthday. According to the Death and Funeral Register of Vänersborg, the cause of death was a cold. The funeral took place in Linköping.[163] However, Lovisa Augusta is not listed in the Cemetery Archive of Linköping, which indicates that she was not buried there.[164] It seems probable that Lovisa Augusta's mother had her body embalmed and transported to Onsjö to be set to rest with her family in their mortuary chapel. This hypothesis is supported by a macabre incident that occurred 121 years later. On September 15, 1959, the following article appeared in the local newspaper Elfsborgs Läns Annonsblad:

Grave defilers of Onsjö still at large

The perpetrators of the senseless violation of graves in the Haij mortuary chapel at the entailed estate of Onsjö in the parish of Vassända-Naglum, were still at large last Monday. The police department of Vänersborg has not been able to find any clues, and since the chapel is somewhat remote, no one has seen or heard anything. Two tombs have been opened; an embalmed corpse has been forced to sit up supported with a stake, while two skulls have been impaled on fence poles.

The police assume that the defilement of the graves was committed at night, when the perpetrators ran a lower risk of being discovered. The grave chapel is located in the woods about 50 meters from the road leading from Överby to the entailed estate.

The chapel has doors made of sheet metal and is locked, secured by a strong crossbar and a stable padlock. The lock has resisted all attempts to be broken, and the perpetrators entered by bending open the lower corner of one of the doors in order to crawl in through a hole.

The chapel housed 16 coffins. Two of them were opened, and an embalmed corpse was severely mishandled. A long stake was pushed under its legs which were then bent up towards the abdomen.

Interior of Onsjö mortuary chapel after the defiling.
Photo from 1959, Museum of Vänersborg.

A large limestone slab on the floor, one meter wide and 7-8 centimeters thick, covers a cavity in the floor, which contains skeletal remains. Two skulls have been taken from this cavity, and an additional skull was removed from one of the coffins. Two of the skulls were discovered, impaled on fence poles at the gate near the road. The third skull was thrown on the ground below.

This is not the first incident involving defilement of the grave chapel. Evidence of tampering was observed during the course of the summer, indicating someone's intent to force entry.

No tools have been found at the chapel, and the police regard it as evident that only fence poles were used to commit the crime. Obviously, more than one person has participated in the violation. The heavy limestone slab is impossible to move using the strength of only one person.

No clues have been found, but the police hope that someone may have observed the individuals who committed this heinous crime. What has happened is completely inexplicable – it is absolutely meaningless. It is considered unlikely that the perpetrators were looking for valuables. ...

One month later, the police arrested three boys, two of them 14 and one 15 years of age. These boys admitted that they defiled the graves. Another 15 years later, in 1974, the mortuary chapel was emptied and all coffins and urns were transported to the graveyard of Vassända-Naglum, where they were interred.[165]

After the defiling of the graves, my sister and I definitely remember that there were discussions about the fact that one of the dead bodies was dressed in a bridal gown. However, we have not been able to find any newspaper articles or letters to the editor confirming this fact. Maybe *Cajsa's* tale simply became the topic of the day in our family? The boys who committed the defiling must now be in their 70's, but the police records containing their names remain confidential. All the people who were involved in the transportation of the deceased from the mortuary chapel to their final resting place at Vassända-Naglum graveyard have now passed away. As a result, no one living can confirm that the embalmed corpse was wrapped in a bridal gown. It is also impossible to prove that Lovisa Augusta pined away due to grief, following the cancellation of her wedding three years earlier. Perhaps she simply died of a severe cold as stated in the Death and Funeral Register? It is possible that she was laid to rest in her unused bridal gown because it was the most splendid piece of clothing in her possession. The tale of her fate may have been embellished with more elaborate details each time it was retold among the employees in the stables and the kitchen of the estate.

However, it was not only the crown prince that *Cajsa Andersdotter* met during her year at Onsjö. She also met a farmhand by the name of *Sven Andersson*, who would soon awaken her interest. The two probably became acquainted already during their first weeks at Onsjö since – on Sunday, November 14, 1841, when nine newly employed from the estate visited the parish office together to report their moving in – *Sven* stood immediately behind *Cajsa* in line,[166] and at the Catechetical Hearing, which was probably held a few weeks later, they sat together and were listed directly after one another in the register.[167] But who was this farmhand named *Sven Andersson*?

Chapter 4:
Sven Andersson's family

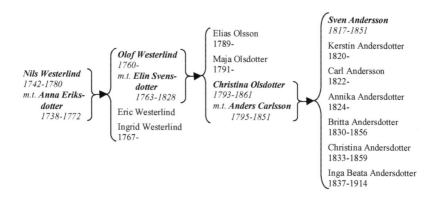

The family within view

The manor of Onsjö, where *Cajsa Andersdotter* and *Sven Andersson* were employed, was located on the western slope of the river Göta Älv. From the main building, there was an unobstructed view of the river, the farms, and the wide fields on the opposite side of the water. Some three kilometers away, the hill Hunneberg formed the horizon of the panorama. The hill has an extraordinary shape, raising vertically about 90 meters high. Its flat, upper surface is covered with forest, lakes and marshes. In the 18th and 19th centuries, a few, isolated cottages were located on the hill. Today, no one resides there. Instead, the hill functions as a recreational area and a royal hunting ground. Along the sides of the hill there are several so-called "klev" (= cleft), natural ravines where footsteps of men through centuries have formed steep paths up the hill. Some of these eroded pathways were eventually transformed into narrow roads.

One of the clefts, which still only offers a walking path up the hill, is Aleklev, just north of the church of Västra Tunhem. From his work place at Onsjö, Sven could see the church tower extend beyond the greenery beneath the dark hillside. Perhaps, he could

The Parishes of Västra Tunhem and Norra Björke.
Detail from map of Väne Judicial District 1895.[168]

3 km

1. Aleklev
2. Bredäng
3. Bryggum
4. Börsle
5. Forstena
6. Grinsjö

7. Gärdet under Berget
8. Herrstad Haregården
9. Hårrum
10. Jönsberg
11. Mossen under
    Gudmundsgården

12. Onsjö manor
13. Trohult
14. Västbjörke Nilsgården
15. Önafors
16. Östbjörke

Part of Hunneberg as seen from Onsjö.[169]

even catch a slight glimpse of the hill cottage just above the cleft, where he was born. His parents, along with several of his little sisters, still lived there. Surely, he must sometimes have straightened his back, resting a minute from work. Wiping his forehead with the back of his hand, he gazed at the far away hill. Maybe he should visit his family some Sunday, when he was free from work? Would he dare ask that pretty chamber maid if she wanted to join him? Surely, his parents would be just as fond of her as he was. If he could just gather up enough courage to ask her to marry him ...

It was not just *Sven Andersson* who had grown up on the hillside of Hunneberg. His mother and father and their forefathers, as far back as we can trace the family, had all lived on or around the hill. *Sven's* father, *Anders Carlsson*, was born in 1795 at Jönsberg, in the Parish of Gärdhem, eight kilometers southwest of Hunneberg. [170] His parents, *Carl Persson* and *Kjerstin Andersdotter*, did not have a farm of their own, since *Carl's* name does not appear in the Tax Register.[171] He probably worked as a servant for one of the farmers at Jönsberg, so *Anders* must have grown up under poor circumstances. In his teens, he himself began to work as a farmhand, at different farms in the neighborhood. Like most young servants, he changed employers annually,[172] until, in 1815, he applied for a position with a farmer by the name of Olle Svensson at Nybygget by Hårrum, just below the southwestern slope of Hunneberg.[173] There he remained for two years, and he had a very special reason to do so. Nybygget was located next to the manor Hårrum, where the Cavalry Captain Jacob Karlström at the same time had hired two farmhands and six maids to tend to his gardens and house. Most probably, *Anders* happened to encounter one or another of them every day, and one of the maids soon caught his interest. Her name was *Christina Olofsdotter* or, more informally, *Stina Olsdotter*.[174] Many years later, *Cajsa Andersdotter* told her granddaughter *Elin* some details that do not appear in the Church Registers: *Stina* was a very beautiful girl, and *Anders* was not the only man to fall in love with her. He had a rival, the son of a rich farmer, but *Stina* did not choose the man with the most money, but instead, the man she loved. On September 29, 1816, *Anders* and *Stina* asked to have the banns published, and on the second day of Christmas they were married. [175]

Now, dear reader, you may ask what happened to *Anders* and *Stina* after their wedding and how they, twenty-five years later, ended up living in a hillside cottage above Aleklev, but before revealing the details of that story, let me first tell you about *Stina's* background, which is much more complicated and confusing than the personal details of her husband, *Anders*.

A puzzle with missing pieces

One problem tracing *Stina's* ancestors backwards into the past is that no Catechetical Hearing Registers are preserved in Västra Tunhem Parish from the time before 1813. This makes it impossible to systematically trace a family from year to year in order to see when various family members were born, moved, married and died. Lacking those essential registers, all we can do is search the Birth and Baptism Registers, the Marriage Registers, and the Death and Funeral Registers, which had been kept since 1688, although, even if we examine them page by page, we cannot be sure of finding all members of a family, particularly since there are obviously entries missing in the early registers. In the Relocation Registers the pastors only listed moves in and out of the parish. They did not include details concerning relocations between farms in the area. As a result, it is not possible to trace the movements of farmhands and maids between different masters. The Tax Registers, which were kept as a basis for tax collection, offer certain continuity, since they were renewed every year, but only the master of each household was identified by name. On some occasions, the name of a child or a farmhand may be noted in the margin of the page. When trying to find information about *Stina's* family, there are pieces of information missing, and we can not be sure that the pieces that we do find fit together to offer a complete picture.

In January of 1742 a boy was born at Bredäng in Norra Björke Parish some five kilometers south of Hunneberg. *Pär* was the name of the boy's father, but the pastor seems to have regarded the name of the mother so unimportant, that it was unnecessary to write it down. All he wrote in the Birth and Baptism Register aside from birth year and month was: "Pär's child in Bredäng – Nils".[176] Many years later, *Nils* himself reported that his parents' names were *Pär Jonson* and *Elin Olofsdotter*.[177] Since there is no Pär Jonsson under Bredäng in the Tax Registers from the 1740's, we can conclude that *Nils'* father did not own or lease a farm of his own, but must have been employed as a farmhand.[178]

In the 18th century, the prospects of the sons of servants were not great. Generally, they had to serve as farmhands for farmers in the area for a number of years. Eventually, with some luck, they might be able to lease a cottage and a small field, paying the rent in days of work. It seems that such a slow way of becoming self-sufficient did not suit *Nils*. The reason was probably that he, already as a teenager, had started to keep company with a girl, four years his senior, by the name of *Anna Eriksdotter*.[3] She came from Östbjörke next to Hunneberg,[179] where her father *Eric Larsson Wärn* farmed a small homestead.[180] Earlier, young couples like *Nils* and *Anna* had to wait for several years before they could get married, since, according to the National Law of 1734, the minimum age for marriage was 21 years for men and 15 years for women. Recently, however, the age limit for a man had been lowered to 18, under the condition that he could support a family. *Nils* and *Anna* would, therefore, be able to get married as soon as *Nils* could fulfill this requirement, but to be employed as a farmhand was not considered good enough to meet this standard. What else could he do?

In 1756, a war had broken out in Europe. On the one side stood Prussia and Great Britain-Hannover, on the other Austria, France, Russia and Spain. In Sweden, after the death of King Karl XII in 1718, Parliament had seized power from the Royal House. Now, the ruling party, the so-called Hats, saw a chance to regain the parts of Pomerania which Karl XII had lost to Prussia. By joining Prussia's antagonists, they calculated, it should be possible to gain a share, once the country had been conquered. Sweden participated in the war from 1757 to 1762, but things did not turn out the way the Hats had hoped. The results at the end of the war were quite unsatisfactory. Sweden had not gained one inch of land but had lost thirty thousand soldiers to diseases and military actions, in addition to a loss of sixty-two million riksdaler in war costs. The country was now on the verge of economic ruin.

---

[3] This is an example of the puzzle that occurs when Catechetical Hearing Registers are missing: When Nils and Anna were married in 1760, both are said to come from the parish. The name of Anna's father is said to be Eric. When Nils' and Anna's daughter Ingrid was born in 1767, Anna's last name is confirmed to be Ericsdotter. When Anna died in 1772, her parents' names are given as Erik Larsson and Marit Bengtsdotter, and Anna's age is said to be 34 years. With this information we can assume that she was probably born around 1738. According to the Birth Register, only one Anna Eriksdotter was born in the parish between 1735 and 1740, namely Eric Wärn's daughter Anna. If the accuracy of the Death Register of 1772 and the Birth Register of 1735-40 can be trusted, Eric Wärn must have been the father of Anna, and his complete name must have been Eric Larsson Wärn.

The regiments of the Swedish army were divided into companies, which were units of 150 soldiers. Each company consisted of six corporalships with 24 soldiers under the command of a corporal. The third corporalship of Väne Company in the regiment of Västgöta-Dal, recruited their soldiers from the parishes of Norra Björke and Väne-Åsaka. In the campaign against Prussia, 14 of the 25 soldiers of the corporalship perished. It was the duty of the farmers of the corresponding file to recruit their replacements. If they failed, they were forced to pay fines or even serve as replacement soldiers themselves. For *Nils*, this presented an opportunity. On April 11, 1760, he was enrolled as a soldier in the file of Västbjörke Nilsgården, just one kilometer away from his parents' home. His height was recorded to be 167 centimeters, and to give a more mature impression of himself, he claimed to be 19 years old, even though he was actually only 18. He was given the soldier's name Westerlind (sometimes spelt Westerling), probably associated with the name of the file Västbjörke. As soon as the agreement was made, he moved to the soldier's croft, and as a result, by the young age of 18, he already had his own dwelling, which included a barn and a piece of land to farm. Furthermore, the farmers of the file were obliged to supply him with seed for sowing and firewood, and when time came for plowing, it was his right to borrow a horse. Nor did he have to feel alone in the croft. *Anna Eriksdotter* soon moved in with him,[181] and on December 28 of the same year they were married.[182]

As I have already mentioned, it is difficult to trace a family from year to year without access to Catechetical Hearing Registers, but in 1766 the Tax Registers were complemented to contain not only the number of employees, but also the number of children and elderly in each household. We can now see that *Nils* and *Anna* after six years of marriage had two children, but since they are not listed in the Birth Register, at this point we do not know their names. There were also two elderly exceeding 63 years of age living in the croft.[183] The following year, one of the elderly passed away.[184] We can guess that it must have been *Nils'* father, since a later register reveals that his mother was then still alive.[185] The same year, *Nils* and *Anna* had a third child, a daughter called Ingrid.[186] In a General Muster in Vänersborg on September 16, *Nils* was approved by the Regimental Officer as a permanently enlisted soldier.[187]

As you already know, in 1772 and 1773, southern Sweden was hit by severe crop failures. Poor people were debilitated by starvation. Many of them died in infectious diseases, particularly dysentery. One of the victims of dysentery was *Nils'* wife *Anna*, who died on December 9, 1772, at the young age of 34.[188] Still suffering from sorrow over having lost his life companion, *Nils* must now have faced severe practical problems. Who would look after his three children, who were between five and twelve years of age? Who would tend to his aging mother? He himself had to take care of the farm and also participate in military exercises to which he was regularly called. The most obvious solution was to find a new wife, which *Nils* succeeded in doing in less than two years. On October 3, 1774, he married a girl named Elin Olofsdotter.[189] The following fall, she bore him a son, whom they called Pär after *Nils'* deceased father.[190] However, within a few months, the newly born died of an unknown disease.[191]

On June 17, 1778, Nils participated in another General Muster in Vänersborg. According to the roll he was commanded to the Carlsten Fortress,[192] a powerful stronghold on the island of Marstrand in the outer archipelago thirty kilometers northwest of Gothenburg. The erection of the fortress was initiated when Sweden had captured the provinces of Skåne and Bohuslän from Denmark in 1658, and although it was recaptured by Denmark/Norway twice within the following sixty years, both times it was returned to Sweden in the peace agreements. Thus, Sweden could continue expanding and reinforcing the fortress. In 1772, when Gustav III had seized power from Parliament and decided to rearm the country as a preparation for new wars, it was decided that the fortress be set in full military stand-by. This must have included reinforced manning, which may explain why Nils was commanded there.

What happened now is unclear. According to a note in the General Muster roll of 1785, *Nils'* health faltered during his time at Carlsten Fortress. He was discharged from the regiment [193] and was forced to leave the soldier's croft, where he and his family had lived for eighteen years.[194] Instead, in January, 1781, a new soldier filled his place and took over the croft.[195] What happened to *Nils* and his family remains a mystery.

One surprise after another

On January 20, 1781, at about the same time that we loose track of *Nils Westerlind* and his family, the farmers of the file Hoghem Östergård in the parish of Tanum, in the northern part of the province of Bohuslän, succeeded in enlisting a new soldier for the Bohuslän Light Dragoon Regiment. His name was *Olof Westerlind* and he was 172 centimeters tall. When it comes to age, he claimed to be 23, which would have placed his birth in the year 1758, but according to later documents he was born in 1760.[196] It was obviously important to appear old enough to be accepted as a dragoon. Not until the following year, this new dragoon moved to Tanum, and according to the Relocation Register he arrived from the neighboring parish Kville "with wife and child".[197] In June of 1783 he participated in his first General Muster, which was held at Backamo military exercise grounds south of the town of Uddevalla. There he was accepted and permanently enlisted as a dragoon.[198] According to the roll from the muster, he originally came from the province of Västergötland, not from Bohuslän, as one would expect. In a letter, which I will return to later, Assistant Vicar Brunius in Tanum claimed that *Olof* was born in Tunhem.

Several facts support the hypothesis that the dragoon *Olof Westerlind* was the son of the soldier *Nils Westerlind*:

- *Olof* was born in Tunhem, and Västbjörke where *Nils* lived was part of the Tunhem church district.
- *Olof* was born the same or almost the same year as *Nils'* oldest child, the name of whom we do not know.

- We have not found any other person than *Nils* by the name of Westerlind in Tunhem at the time that *Olof* was born.

- In the General Muster roll no son-name is noted for *Olof*, which indicates that Westerlind was an inherited family name, rather than a newly awarded soldier's name.

But if *Olof* was really the son of *Nils*, we are faced with a difficult question:

- Why had *Olof* already as a teenager moved eighty kilometers away from his family in Tunhem to Kville? Did it have anything to do with the fact that *Nils* was transferred to Carlsten Fortress in 1778?

To sum up facts, it is probable – but not completely certain – that *Olof* was the son of *Nils*. On the other hand, it can be regarded as certain, that *Olof*, a number of years later, became the grandfather of *Cajsa's* husband *Sven Andersson*. Therefore, we will continue to trace *Olof's* rather intricate fate.

So far, we have learned that *Olof* moved to Tanum in 1782, where he was permanently enlisted as a dragoon. The next piece of information that I have found regarding *Olof* comes, surprisingly enough, from the Birth Register of Västra Tunhem. On November 1, 1784, he and his wife Karin Andersdotter became the parents of a son, Jacob. His place of birth is Grinsjö, a cottage on Hunneberg.[199] Obviously, the family had moved away from Tanum, but they are not registered in the Tanum Transition Register. We find an explanation in the earlier mentioned letter from Assistant Vicar Brunius in Tanum who writes:

The soldier Olof Westerlind ... has ... in 1783 ... rapidly left town, without requiring a transition certificate from the parish office.

Obviously, *Olof* and Karin had fled Tanum head over heels. We ask ourselves why.

One of the witnesses at Jacob's baptism was *Elin Svensdotter*. Our next surprise occurs when we learn that, on July 8, 1787, about two and a half years after the baptism, *Olof* calls for banns to marry her. The wedding took place at Grinsjö on August 4 of the same year, which must have been as early as possible, considering that the banns must first be read from the pulpit in the local church three Sundays in a row. For almost all wedding couples, the names of the parents are given in the Marriage Register, but not for *Olof*. Was he trying to hide his origin from the pastor?[200] And how could he suddenly marry another woman? Had his first wife died? Also in this case, we find further information in the letter from Assistant Vicar Brunius:

> *They say that he* (Olof Westerlind) *has found his way to Uddevalla, where rumors claim that he has married, since a formal notification of missing had been made after his escaped wife, who, in the certificate with which Westerlind arrived here in 1782, is called Karin Carlsdotter.*

Olof's first wife, Karin Andersdotter (or Carlsdotter as she is probably erroneously called in the letter from the assistant vicar) had evidently escaped from her husband after bearing him at least two children! Why did she do that? Was *Olof* not a good husband? Was he gone on military assignments for extended periods of time? Did life in the isolated cottage in the forests of Hunneberg become unbearable? Did she long for her family in Kville? Did she take the children with her when she escaped? Unfortunately, we have only questions, and no answers. What we know for certain is that the notification of the escaped wife as missing, according to the National Law of 1734, must have been read from the pulpits of the churches in all of Väne Judicial District, including neighboring parishes, and that *Olof* must have waited an entire year before he could have a letter of divorce issued, in order to be permitted to marry again.[201] This must have been a lengthy delay for *Olof* and for his new fiancée.

But who was his new wife, *Elin Svensdotter*? She was born at Trohult on Hunneberg in 1763,[202] and had lived there all of her childhood and youth together with her parents, *Sven Pehrsson* and *Ingeborg Torstensdotter*, and her three siblings.[203] The cottage Grinsjö, where *Olof's* son Jacob was born and where he and *Elin* were married, was also located on Hunneberg and was probably regarded as Trohult's closest neighbor, although they were separated by four kilometers of forest and marshes. Then again, we can not be absolutely sure that *Olof* had actually lived at Grinsjö after returning to Tunhem, since his name can not be found in the Tax Registers. If he did reside there, then he could not have been responsible for his own household.

As soon as the wedding between *Olof* and *Elin* was completed, they moved to Uddevalla. The rumor that Olof had "found his way to Uddevalla" and that he had married was, thus, almost correct. For *Elin* it must have been an overwhelming experience to leave her parents' isolated cottage in the forest and move to a town with streets, rows of houses, and even a harbor open to the infinite Atlantic Ocean. Surely, she would have liked to stroll around and observe everything, but there was no time for that. On the very same day that *Olof* reported their moving in at the church office,[204] *Elin* bore their first child, a son, who was given the name Jeremias.[205] At the end of the year, a wedding took place back in *Olof's* birth parish Norra Björke. A cottager named Eric Westerlind married a girl called Catharina Svensdotter Hallberg. The names of the parents of the bridegroom are clearly written: *Nils Westerlind* and *Anna Ericsdotter*.[206] Obviously, Eric was the name of *Olof's* younger brother.

In March of 1788, Uddevalla was struck by an epidemic of smallpox. Before the year was over, 79 people had died of the disease, all children, ten years or less. One of the cases occurred on June 19. The victim was a boy named Jeremias. In the Death Register, his father is said to be a dragoon named Anders Westerlind,[207] but since Jeremias was an unusual name and the age of the child differs only two months from that of *Olof's* and *Elin's* son, we have reason to believe that the pastor inadvertently recorded the wrong first name of the father. It is highly likely that it was *Olof* and *Elin* who had lost their son.

One week after the death of Jeremias, *Olof* participated in another General Muster at Backamo. After his name, there is a note in the roll: "Legs injured, requests and is given dismissal".[208] We do not know the extent of *Olof's* injury or how it occurred, but as the saying goes, "Every cloud has a silver lining." Thanks to his dismissal, *Olof* did not have to face the Danish/Norwegian army who would, a few weeks later, attack Bohuslän from Norway. In the battle of Kvistrum north of Uddevalla, on September 29, 1788, five Swedish soldiers were killed in action, while another 61 were wounded. This was the only violent confrontation in the earlier mentioned "show war" between Sweden and Denmark/Norway.

The time that *Olof* and *Elin* lived in Uddevalla was brief, less than two years. On May 20, 1788, they moved back to her parents at Trohult in Tunhem.[209] A little over two months later, *Elin* bore them a second son, who was named Elias.[210] Then the family must have moved to Börsle, one kilometer south of Hunneberg, since this is where she bore two additional children, the daughters Maja, born on August 5, 1791,[211] and *Christina Uliana*, born on September 26, 1793.[212] The information about the birth place of *Christina Uliana* can be found in later Catechetical Hearing Registers, but in the Birth and Baptism Register, the pastor, instead of a place of birth, has written some indecipherable words:

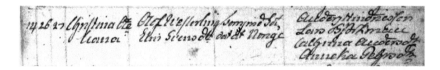

What does it say in the second last column? It seems to end in "åt Norige" (= "towards Norway" or "for Norway") but what are the preceding words? If you, dear reader, can interpret the pastor's handwriting, please contact me. At any rate, this is the last piece of information that I have found regarding *Olof*, and the reason will soon appear: Just like his first wife, *Olof* had vanished! The brief note in the Birth and Baptism Register, most probably, summarizes what *Olof's* wife told the pastor about his disappearance.

Although Västra Tunhem was part of the diocese of Skara, it appears that cases regarding divorce were handled by the Cathedral Chapter of Gothenburg. Before the Notification of Missing of an escaped spouse was announced from the church pulpits, the chapter must contact "the clergy and other persons concerned" to inquire if they knew where the missing person dwelled.[213] In *Olof's* case, the question was first directed to the Assistant Vicar in Tanum, whose answer I have already partially cited. A second inquiry was directed to the pastor in Uddevalla, but he knew as little as his colleague in Tanum about *Olof's* whereabouts.[4] It soon proved that announcing his Notification of Missing from the church pulpits gave an equally meager result. *Olof* was nowhere to be found.

Olof's restless and unpredictable life makes you wonder. Why did he move so suddenly and so far several times? One explanation could be that he was a generally restless person, but there is also another explanation close at hand. What if he fled to avoid heavy, corporal labor? Here are some observations supporting the latter hypothesis:

– When *Olof* was 18 years old, his father was transferred to Carlsten Fortress. The family remained at the soldier's croft in Västbjörke, and *Olof*, being the oldest son, probably had the responsibility of taking over the farming. If he disliked corporal labor, he would gladly have passed this role off to his younger brother Eric. It was simply a matter of figuring out how to accomplish this. Running away might be a solution! Could this be the reason why *Olof* suddenly turned up in Kville in northern Bohuslän, 80 kilometers from home, and that he much later, when he marries *Elin Svensdotter*, refuses to reveal his parents' name for the pastor?

– In Kville *Olof* met a girl and a baby was soon on its way. In order to be able to marry before turning 21, he had to prove that he could support a family. Accepting an enlistment in the army was one way of solving this problem, but why did *Olof* wait an entire year before moving into his soldier's croft in

---

[4] The answers of both clergymen are available in the supplement "Letters regarding the disappearance of Olof Westerlind".

Tanum? Farming his lot there could support both him, his wife, and their child. Could it have been more comfortable to remain where he was, probably in the home of his in-laws, for as long as possible?

- *Olof* did not remain in his soldier's croft in Tanum more than one year. Then he eventually fled head over heals back to Västra Tunhem accompanied by his wife and child. What drove him from the croft? Was it his dislike of farm work?

- After about a year in Västra Tunhem his wife left him, and he remarried *Elin Svensdotter*. We do not know how he made a living during this time, but there is a good chance that he had to help with the daily chores at the cottage where he was lodging. Was this why he moved to Uddevalla so abruptly?

- How *Olof* could pay for room and board for himself and his family in Uddevalla remains a mystery. It was the croft in Tanum, from which he had fled, that formed his salary from the regiment. Could there have been a conflict regarding this that caused *Olof* to resign from his military position, using his "injured legs" as an excuse?

- As soon as *Olof* had been dismissed from the regiment, he moved with *Elin* to his in-laws on Hunneberg and later on to Börsle south of the hill. He did not farm an estate of his own, so we must assume that he worked as a farmhand. If the hypothesis that *Olof* abhorred heavy, manual labor is correct, this could explain why he, at the age of 33, disappeared, leaving *Elin* to care for their three children on her own.

What happened to *Elin Svensdotter* during the following twenty years we do not know, but in the first preserved Catechetical Hearing Register of Västra Tunhem we find her again. The year is 1813, and she now lives in the hill cottage above Aleklev.[5]

---

[5] *Elin Svensdotter* is from now on said to be born in "Dahl", which is short for Dalsland, but this must be due to a misunderstanding that spread from register to register. Name, birth date, and the connection to her daughter

Three years later her newly wed daughter *Stina Olsdotter* (the middle name Uliana no longer appears in the registers) and her husband *Anders Carlsson* joined her there.[214] *Stina* and *Anders* soon moved out, but *Elin* stayed in the hill cottage for the remainder of her life. When she had reached the age of 57, as a last surprise, she married the farmhand Johannes Andersson, who was 19 years her junior.[215] He was born in Grinsjö, the neighbor cottage of *Elin's* childhood home. It is therefore quite possible that she had babysat her new husband when he was young! In the Marriage Register, the pastor has added in very decorative writing:

> *Wife divorced from her escaped husband through court and Cathedral Chapter decision. The children nothing to claim.*

The Cathedral Chapter had, obviously, declared *Elin* divorced from *Olof Westerlind*, who through this legal decision had lost his rights to any property in his former wife's estate. When a divorced woman remarried, the children from the previous marriage, however, had the right to claim the inheritance after their father. In this case, 27 years had passed since *Olof* disappeared, and in the simple hill cottage, there can hardly have been anything left to inherit after him. This explains why the pastor has made the note "The children nothing to claim".

Elin and her new husband Anders Carlsson lived together for eight years. They were both sickly and impoverished.[216] In the spring of 1828, Anders died of dropsy.[217] On December 13 of the same year, *Elin* finally passed away on the very same hill and in the very same forest where she had first seen the light of day 65 years earlier.[218]

Now, one final question remains before we can return to the story about *Sven Andersson's* parents *Stina Olsdotter* and *Anders Carlsson*. *Stina* was born as *Christina Uliana Olofsdotter* around

---

Christina Uliana proves that she must still be the *Elin Svensdotter* from Trohult.

the time of her father's disappearance. What happened to her then? By tracing her through the church registers from adult age and backwards, we find that she grew up as a foster child to Erik Olofsson and his wife Anna Andersdotter in Assarebyn of Färgelanda Parish in Dalsland, about forty kilometers from the place where she was born.[219] She arrived there some time between 1795 and 1801, which indicates that she was between two and eight years old when she was brought there. Erik Olofsson at the time was around 40 and his wife 13 years older. They had no children of their own – or at least no children living at home – but employed a farmhand and a maid to help them. Why was *Stina* left to foster parents, and why did she end up so far away from home? Once again we have no answers but can only speculate. When *Olof Westerlind* disappeared, *Stina's* mother *Elin Svensdotter* was left alone without anyone to provide for the family. Maybe she was unable to take care of the children by herself? Maybe the family in Färgelanda was her relatives, although I have not been able to confirm that this was the case? Anyway, *Stina* remained at the farm of her foster parents in Assarebyn during her entire youth, except for a short period of time,[220] when she worked as a maid at Skriketorp in the same parish.[221] There is, however, no doubt that she was the biological daughter of *Elin Svensdotter* and *Olof Westerlind*. At the age of twenty, she decided to return to Västra Tunhem,[222] where she later lived for some time with her mother *Elin Svensdotter*.[223] As additional evidence, the family name Westerlind appears after her name in a later church register.[224]

In Tunhem *Stina* worked as a maid at several different farms: for the Lieutenant-Colonel Gustaf Liljehorn of Forstena 1813-14,[225] for Nils Andersson at Herrstad Haregården 1814-15[226] and, finally, for the Cavalry Captain Jacob Karlström at the manor of Hårrum 1815-16.[227] This is where she became a neighbor to the farmhand *Anders Carlsson,* who was soon to become her husband.

In the death grip of poverty

As I have already mentioned on page 72, *Anders* and *Stina* had the banns published on September 29, 1816. The same week, their employment contract expired, and *Stina* moved to the hill cottage at Aleklev, to live with her mother.[228] *Anders* joined her a short time later, most probably after their wedding on the second day of Christmas the same year. On September 18, 1817, their first child was born. He was named *Sven*, presumably after his grandmother's father *Sven Persson* of Trohult.[229] The following year, the family left Aleklev to move to a leased cottage at Mossen under Gundmundsgården just southwest of Hunneberg.[230] Here, five children were born:

– Kerstin, born on February 16, 1820,[231]

– Carl, born on April 15, 1822,[232]

– Annika, born on January 6, 1824,[233]

– Anna Stina, born on November 14, 1825,[234] died from measles on November 29, 1836,[235] and

– Britta, born on October 18, 1828,[236] died from pertussis (also known as whooping cough) on January 4, 1829.[237]

When *Stina's* mother and her husband had died, the family moved back to the hill cottage at Aleklev, where another five children were born:

– Britta, born on June 10, 1830,[238] died from dropsy on September 24, 1856,[239]

– Christina, born on January 30, 1833,[240] died from tuberculosis and wasting on December 18, 1859,[241]

– Inga Beata, born on December 15, 1835,[242] died on November 23, 1836,[243] and the twins

– Inga Beata, born November 22, 1837,[244] and

– Anna Christina, born on November 23, 1837,[245] died from dropsy on February 20, 1853.[246]

Out of eleven children, two died while they were still toddlers, two when they were teenagers, and two around the age of twenty-five. Without a doubt, malnourishment was the leading cause of both wasting (= weight loss) and dropsy (= swelling of belly and/or legs). With a growing family, there was an increasing number of mouths to feed, and *Anders'* income as a temporary farmhand, in addition to what the family could harvest, was insufficient. During their years at Mossen, Anders diligently worked at different farms from Monday through Saturday, and on Sundays he served as organ blower in the church. [247] A typical annual salary for this Sabbath task was one loaf of bread from each farmer in the parish and one day's offerings from the church. When the family had moved back to the hill cottage at Aleklev, their suffering became even worse. Anders had to seek steady employment as a farmhand, which meant that he had to be present at his employer's farm all week, with the consequence that he had to leave his family in order to reside at his work place. For example, during the years 1832-34, he was registered as living at Anders Andersson's farm in Bryggum no. 3, although the distance to his family home in Aleklev was less than three kilometers. [248]

In 1834, *Sven Andersson*, the oldest son in the family, moved away from home to work as a farmhand for the foundry proprietor Emanuel Nordström of Önafors in Vassända-Naglum Parish, immediately west of Göta Älv. He was now 17 years old. When he reported the transition at the church office, he not only called himself *Sven Andersson,* but also added that his family name was Glädje (= Joy). [249] At about the same time, his father presented the same family name in the Catechetical Hearing in Bryggum. Glädje was a typical soldier's name, but neither *Anders* nor *Sven* were soldiers, and I have not been able to find anyone with this name earlier in the family. On the other hand, everyone was still more or less free to adopt any family name he wanted in the 19th century, and it is quite possible that father and son had agreed on calling themselves Glädje. Perhaps it was in an attempt to brighten up the otherwise dismal situation of the family? However, these two instances seem to be the only occasion when anyone in the family called himself Glädje. Maybe the name appeared as mockery, when two of the children in the family died in the course of one week the following year? Much later the name Glädje would appear again, but then as a shunned nickname for some people in the family.

After three years of labor at Önafors,[250] *Sven* left the household of proprietor Nordström and moved back to the eastern side of the river, where he found employment as a farmhand at Anders Bengtsgården under Bryggum no. 3.[251] This was the very same farm, where his father had worked three years earlier. The following year, *Sven* worked at Gärdet in the file Berget no. 11,[252] but then he decided to move back to Vassända-Naglum Parish on the western side of the river. On November 14, 1841, he reported to the church office of Västra Tunhem, that he was going to work as a farmhand for the noble family Haij at Onsjö Manor. There, he would soon meet his future wife, *Cajsa Andersdotter*.[253]

Sven's parents and several of his siblings still lived in the hill cottage above Aleklev. In spite of his father's, *Anders Carlsson's*, efforts to make a living on temporary employment, the family was impoverished. On May 23, 1849, a devastating fire broke out in the town of Lidköping, 50 kilometers north-east of Västra Tunhem. Almost 800 people were left without homes.[254] The reconstruction of the town required many working hands. In Västra Tunhem about ten people requested relocation certificates to go to Lidköping. *Anders* was the first one. He left his home on June 2, 1849, not to return until April 3, 1850.[255] Even if he was forced to stay away from his family for ten months, this must have been a more certain way of earning an income than his usual day-to-day commissions. The following year, *Anders* was killed in an accident, which we will get back to in the following chapter.

Anders' widow, *Stina Olsdotter*, remained in the hillside cottage during all of the 1850's, but this was not a happy phase of her life. As a pauper she received some support from the parish. Just the same, two of her daughters, Anna Christina and Britta, died of starvation related diseases in 1853 and 1856. The youngest daughter, Inga Beata, moved away from home in 1857, but when the last daughter still residing at home, Christina, also died of starvation ("tuberculosis and wasting") in 1859, Inga Beata returned home to take care of her mother. She remained there until her mother finally passed away on May 31, 1861.[256] According to a note in the hearing register, towards the end of her life, *Stina Olsdotter* turned blind. [257] Most probably the cause was cataracts, which would later affect several of her descendants. *Cajsa Andersdotter*, however, gave another explanation. For lack of fire wood *Stina* used to gather brush in the forest. She was old and bent, and by accident poked out her eyes on the twigs.

After *Stina Olsdotter's* death, her daughter Inga Beata definitely left the hillside cottage at Aleklev. She later married and became Inga Beata Stig. She lived until April 7, 1914,[258] and is the first person in this book to have her picture preserved in a photo.

Inga Beata Andersdotter Stig with her daughter Hilda.

Chapter 5:

Cajsa Andersdotter in Västra Tunhem

Cajsa Andersdotter
1818-1907
m.t. Sven Andersson Glädje
1817-1851

Maria Christina Svensdotter
1844-1918
Johanna Sofia Svensdotter
1846-

The down-side of peace

Sven Andersson and *Cajsa Andersdotter* obviously became attracted to each other within their first weeks at Onsjö Manor. As soon as they found the privacy necessary to get to know each other, they must have discovered how much they had in common: both had grown up in cold, dark hill cottages, both were used to going to bed with an empty stomach, and both had seen siblings die from malnourishment. When their relationship had matured and they started to plan for a future together, they must have agreed on one thing: they were going to give their children a better start in life than they had experienced themselves!

After just three months at Onsjö, *Sven* requested "certificate for becoming a soldier",[259] and it is easy to imagine the motivation of his request. A soldier's croft with some ground to farm and the right to request certain support from the responsible farmers of the file, was surely the best future he and *Cajsa* could imagine, particularly now that the country had been at peace for 28 years. Having to participate in military exercises now and then was an easy sacrifice to make in order to obtain the desirable croft. If only God and the King would see to it that no war broke out, *Sven* would not risk being commanded to some foreign country, perhaps never to return. This was a beautiful dream for their future, but it did not come to pass, at least not during their time at Onsjö. No soldier's croft in the area became vacant, and when the employment year came to an end, in October of 1842, *Cajsa* and *Sven* decided to move together to her parents' home in

Gestad.[260] Perhaps, they thought, they might have better luck there.

As soon as the young couple had settled themselves in *Cajsa's* parents' hill cottage Hagen under Simonstorp, they had the banns published.[261] Their wedding took place on December 16.[262] Now, all they wanted was to find a vacant soldier's croft as soon as possible. *Sven* immediately requested another certificate to become a soldier, but his luck failed in the same way this time.[263] Obviously, peace had its down-side. During the wars of 1757-62, 1788-89, and 1808-09, as many as half of the soldiers of the parishes were killed or captured, and those that had perished had to be replaced by newly enlisted. In times of peace, the situation was different. The soldiers could remain in their crofts until age forced them to resign, and this, of course, made it much more difficult for new, young men to become enlisted. After a few months, however, another possibility surfaced. A croft was free to lease in Västra Tunhem, not far from where *Sven's* parents lived. His father probably contacted the property owner, even before he sent a message to *Sven*. After all, being a tenant crofter was better than serving as a farmhand or a day-to-day worker. *Sven* and *Cajsa* immediately set off to the parish office to request a relocation certificate. This time the pastor made use of the occasion to check their reading skills and their knowledge of Luther's catechism and explanations. After first having listened to *Sven*, he wrote down the grades "well, warrantable, passable" in the Relocation Register. Then it was *Cajsa's* turn. You can imagine how the pastor nodded his head contentedly as he wrote down her grades "well, well, warrantable". Both of them were obviously able to read well, but when it came to reciting Luther's catechism and explanations by heart, *Cajsa's* skills surpassed those of *Sven*.[264]

In October 1843, *Cajsa* and *Sven* left the hill cottage in Gestad. Even if the only room was less crowded, it must have been a sad situation for *Cajsa's* parents. Their youngest son, Johannes, was now the only child remaining at home. Except him and Cajsa, all of their other six children had died. Soon enough, Johannes would also move out to make his own living.[265] The first years he worked as a farmhand for different masters in his home parish Gestad.[266] In 1851, he moved to the peninsula Vänersnäs on the other side of Dalbosjön, the bay of Vänern that reaches down to Vänersborg. The road around the bay from Gestad to Vänersnäs via Vänersborg is about fifty kilometers, which must have been regarded as a long distance in the 1850's, when traveling was achieved by foot or possibly by horse and cart. Across the water, on the other hand, Vänersnäs lay just seven or eight kilometers away and could be clearly seen from Gestad. It is likely that Johannes asked one of the local fishermen to transport him there in his boat.[267] Having served for two years at different farms on Vänersnäs,[268] Johannes returned to Gestad. At least, this is what the pastor wrote in the Relocation Register of Vänersnäs.[269] However, he occurs neither in Gestad Relocation Register, Catechetical Hearing Register or Death Register, so most probably he was offered employment in some other parish at the very last moment and decided to go there instead. As a result, we lose track of him and he disappears from this story.

Cajsa's father, *Anders Olsson*, with the added family name Landgren, was now old and feeble. His lame right arm made it even harder to make a living on a day-to-day basis. In the Catechetical Hearing Register he is classified as a pauper. On March 2, 1853, his days ended. Together with his loved one, *Kerstin Olsdotter*, he had lived in the same hill cottage for 37 years.[270] *Kerstin* was now also to be counted among the paupers of the parish. She survived her husband by eight years and regularly attended Holy Communion.[271] On February 5, 1861, she drew her last breath.[272]

Merchants, farmers, crofters, and cottage dwellers

On November 1, 1843, *Sven* and *Cajsa* reported their move to their new home in Västra Tunhem.[273] The croft was located on land belonging to the farm Persgården in the file of Malöga, on the eastern shore of Göta Älv. For *Sven* and *Cajsa,* it must have felt like returning to the place where they had first met. Onsjö was only two kilometers away on the other side of the river. At the same time, everything was different. They were now husband and wife; they lived together in a cottage of their own, and also had a field of their own to farm. Well, it was not quite their own. They leased both the cottage and the field and had to pay rent in days of work. Nevertheless, it must have felt like a huge step forward. The owner of the land was a man around 55 years of age by the name of Andreas Andersson. He was married and had five children. *Sven* and *Cajsa*, no doubt, did their best to get along well with him.

But life is sometimes more complicated than one can expect. About fifteen years earlier, Parliament had decided that a final agricultural redistribution must be undertaken. This time, the goal was to gather all the land of each farmer into one coherent lot, in order to create ultimate conditions for modernized and rational farming. The reform was known as the "legal redistribution" and was implemented in phases during the following decades.[274] Many farmers did not view this shift as something universally positive, since they did not want to give up fields that their forefathers had farmed for generations. There were, however, also those who gladly traded their lots. One of these was the wholesale merchant Lars Wilhelm Prytz of Överby, on the western side of the river. He was born in Gothenburg, and had travelled extensively both in Europe and America as a young man. Later in his life, he started a wholesale business, and with the profit he made, he bought a number of country estates, one of them being the farm at Överby.[275] Recently, he had also bought a piece of land in the file of Malöga, on the eastern side of the river. In 1835, Prytz wrote to the Governor of the province to request that the land surveyor, Lieutenant Carl Adamsson, be commissioned to implement the legal redistribution of land at Malöga. It is remarkable that Prytz not only requested that redistribution be performed, but also named the land surveyor whom he wanted to fulfill the task. A tempting explanation would be that Adamsson was a friend of Prytz, who therefore expected the outcome of the redistribution to result to his advantage. True or not, the governor conceded to Prytz's request, and in September of the following year, Adamsson arrived at Malöga to redistribute the land. It now appeared that all landowners, except Prytz, objected to the redistribution. The reason was that the south side of the file bordered on the creek Stallbackaån, and "the swampy condition of the land and the damage caused by the water" made it impossible to redistribute the land "without severe suffering for some of the land owners." Adamsson, however, was not to be swayed. In spite of the protests of the land owners, he produced a plan, where each of them was awarded two lots: one less attractive in the swampy area next to the creek, and one more attractive on higher land further away from the areas where water collected. All land owners, except Prytz, refused to accept this plan. Adamsson did not yield, but sent his plan to the Redis-

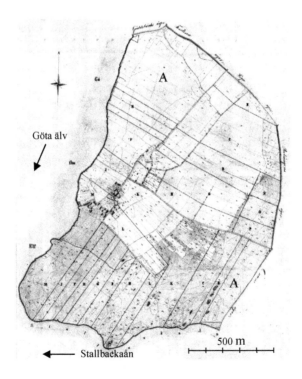

Map of Malöga village with surrounding ground lots
from the legal redistribution in 1839. The lots awarded
to G W Prytz are marked with an A.

tribution Court for a decision. After one round of complaints to the District Court, Adamsson's plan was confirmed. In July of 1839, Adamsson reappeared in Malöga to present the result. It can hardly have come as a surprise that he had awarded Prytz the two lots that were located at the greatest distance from the swampy corner, where the creek Stallbackaån ran out into the river Göta Älv.[276]

Initially, *Sven* and *Cajsa* were not concerned with the redistribution. They farmed their lot and served their days of labor for Andreas Andersson, but soon Prytz began to purchase more of the land under Malöga. This was probably facilitated by the fact that the other land owners were dissatisfied with the lots they had been awarded. For Andreas Andersson there is now a note, "allotment," in the Catechetical Hearing Register. It indicates that he sold his farm in exchange for the promise that he and his wife could remain living in the homestead with certain privileges for the rest of their lives. Most likely, they were assigned a smaller house next to the main building, known as an "allotment." Above Andreas Andersson's name, the names of the new owners of the land are written: "L W Prytz and banks."

The impact of the change of owners soon struck *Sven* and *Cajsa*. The earlier note "Tenant crofters under Andreas Andersson" is now crossed out and replaced by "Cottage dwellers under L W Prytz." The new owner had obviously canceled their lease contract in order to farm all of his land under direct rule. Thus, *Sven* and *Cajsa* were back at square one: their leased croft had turned into a rented cottage. They could no longer produce their own food, and just like their parents, they now had to support themselves with temporary positions of employment.[277]

During the following years, three children saw the light of day:

- *Maria Christina*, born on September 28, 1844, missing in the Birth Register,[278]
- Johanna Sofia, born on February 9, 1846,[279] and
- Anna Beata, born on October 11, 1847.[280]

When Johanna Sofia was baptized, Andreas Andersson and his wife participated as witnesses, so obviously *Sven* and *Cajsa* remained on friendly terms with their previous landlords. Later, the wholesale merchant Prytz assigned his land in Malöga to his son-in-law, the "possessioner and landlord" Lars Casimir Albrecht Ehrengranat,[281] who lived with his family at Gäddebäck, directly north of Malöga.[282] Just like his father-in-law, he refused to lease out any lots, since it had proved to be more profitable to farm the land by means of cheap, hired labor than to lease it out to crofters in exchange for days of work. This second change of owners meant no improvement for *Sven* and *Cajsa*. They also soon met new ordeals. In 1845, western Sweden was struck by crop failure,[283] and in 1850 their youngest daughter died of measles, just two and a half years old.[284]

Death in the creek

Life as a day-to-day worker was hard and unpredictable. During the summer, it was easy to find work at farms in the area. It was not until about fifty years later, that the first agricultural machines would come into use, so hay-making, harvest, threshing, and transports at this time still required many industrious hands. Working days were long. The sun came out before four in the morning and continued to shine until nine in the evening. So far, there were no restrictions on working hours. In winter, it was difficult to find work in the country, but in Trollhättan options were better. There, new industries that required labor all year were being established. For those who lived in Malöga, it took about an hour to walk to the factories in Trollhättan and another hour to return home at the end of the day. Darkness and cold did not make the situation easier.

Tuesday, January 28, 1851, would for ever etch a mark in *Cajsa's* memory. Most likely, she, *Sven*, and *Sven's* father, *Anders Carlsson*, had succeeded in finding temporary employment in one of the new factories. Just like other mornings, she and *Sven* woke up before the crack of dawn to make it to work on time. *Anders* must have set out even earlier from Aleklev. Perhaps his wife *Stina Olsdotter* accompanied him to Malöga to take care of her grand children while their parents were away. *Stina* still had three half grown daughters of her own in the hill cottage at Aleklev, but they were old enough to take care of themselves.

It was evening when *Cajsa, Sven* and *Anders* made their way home. In the darkness they followed the river northwards and had a short distance to go to reach the cottage at Malöga. They only needed to cross the creek Stallbackaån first. The road over the bridge by Hullsjön was a long way around. It was much faster to climb down the river bank and walk across the ice. Many years later, *Cajsa* told *Elin* what happened. When they reached the middle of the creek, the ice suddenly gave way under their feet, and all three plunged into the ice-cold water. In a panic they called for help, but the distance to the village was more than five hundred meters, and no one came to their rescue. *Sven* made a serious effort to help *Cajsa* climb out of the water and on to the ice, but her long skirt was a hindrance. Finally, she was ready to give up and sobbed: "Save yourself!" Sven answered breathlessly: "The children need you more!" After another few attempts, he succeeded in pushing her up onto the ice. She turned around in an attempt to help him, but it was too late. Helpless, she saw him disappear in the black water. His father *Anders* was already gone. Shocked and chilled to the bone she ran the last hundred meters home to the cottage, where *Stina* and the children were waiting. The following Sunday, the funeral for *Sven* and *Anders* was held in the church of Västra Tunhem. This is how *Cajsa* and her mother-in-law *Stina* both became widows at the same time.[285]

One would expect a drowning incident with two victims to appear in the headlines of the local press. At the time of the accident, there was one newspaper in Vänersborg: *Tidning för Wenersborgs stad och län* (= Newspaper for Vänersborg Town and Province), which was issued every Wednesday, but it does not mention a word about the accident.[286] Maybe cottage dwellers were too insignificant to waste any column space? Nineteen years later, the same newspaper presented a wide-ranging obituary after the previous wholesale merchant L W Prytz.

After the accident, only three members remained in *Cajsa's* family: *Cajsa* herself, 32 years, and her daughters *Maria Christina*, 6 years, and Johanna Sofia, 4 years. In the Catechetical Hearing Registers they are described as "impoverished" and "paupers." In the following register[287] the word "cottage dwellers" is crossed out and replaced by "dependent," which must mean that *Cajsa* and the children were no longer allowed to live in the cottage under Persgården, at least not by themselves. On the same page, a number of contract workers are listed together with their families. L W Prytz and later Albrecht Ehrengranat must have needed every square meter they could find to house their many employees. As impoverished dependent tenants, *Cajsa* and the children lived under Persgården for another six years, but on Sunday, August 23, 1857, their lives took a new turn. On this day banns for marriage were published between *Cajsa* and the sawmill worker Jonas Eriksson in Trollhättan.[288]

Chapter 6:

Cajsa Andersdotter at Stavre Mosse

Who was Jonas Eriksson?

This many years later, it is impossible to know how *Cajsa Andersdotter* and Jonas Ericsson met. They may well have known each other already in their youth, since Jonas originally came from Bolstad, which is located directly north of *Cajsa's* home parish of Gestad, in the province of Dalsland. A six year age difference separated the two; still she was 19 when he, at the age of 25, left Bolstad to move to Trollhättan. At any rate, their roads crossed at this point, which is by no means strange, since the distance between Malöga, where *Cajsa* lived as a dependant pauper, and Stavre Mosse, where Jonas rented a dwelling-place, was no more than three kilometers. Even if they did not know each other before, they must immediately have realized that they came from the same area as soon as they heard each other talk. According to *Elin*, *Cajsa* spoke with a heavy Dalsland dialect, and it is highly probable that Jonas did so as well. When they had time to speak in private, they must have also discovered a number of other similarities.

Jonas was born in Bolstad Parish in Dalsland on February 11, 1812.[289] His parents, Erik Hansson and the seven years older Elin Persdotter, were poor day-to-day workers who lived as dependant tenants at Muggerud under Ekarebol. In the Catechetical Hearing Register, the pastor has written, as an explanation to their poverty: "impoverished due to wasting".[290] What kind of mistake they had made, according to the pastor's judgment, we do not know, only that he regarded them as having caused their own misfortune. Jonas was Erik's and Elin's second, but only living child. Their first son, Petter, had died at the age of three already in 1810.[291]

When Jonas was two years old, his father died in a fever,[292] and four years later his mother married the "obviously fragile" farmhand Sven Persson of Muggerud.[293] The following year, Olof had a little sister by the name of Cajsa.[294] For a short period of time (1821-23), we cannot trace the family because pages are missing from the current Catechetical Hearing Register, but in 1824 they re-appear in the next register. By this time, Jonas is listed as a "service boy" at Södra Hagen, while the rest of the family live as dependant tenants at Skälesbyn under Norra Hagen. Jonas must, thus, have left home already at the age of twelve or possibly even earlier.[295] Why did he move away from his parents at such a young age? Did he want to escape from his step-father, or did the parish not allow an able-bodied twelve-year-old to live with his parents as a dependant tenant? We shall never know, but the register offers a tragic picture of the family. The step-father is described as "fragile" and the mother as "paralyzed, for many years fragile".[296]

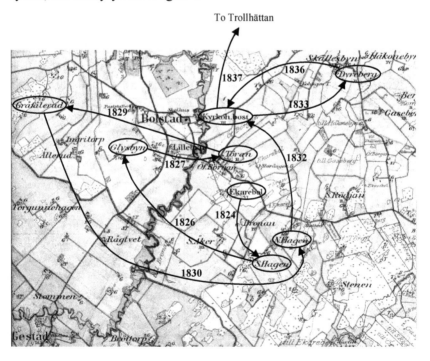

Map illustrating Jonas Eriksson's moves within Bolstad Parish, from the time he was born at Muggerud under Ekarebol in 1812 until he moved to Trollhättan in 1837.

Jonas must have learned to rely on himself at a very young age. From the time he was 12 until the time he was 25, he worked for a number of different employers in Bolstad Parish,[297] first as a service boy and later as a farmhand. His moves between farms are illustrated in the enclosed map.

In 1837, Jonas must have decided to begin a new phase in his life: he acquired a certificate to move to the growing industrial community of Trollhättan.[298] There, the river Göta Älv, which runs from the Lake Vänern to the Atlantic Ocean, passes through a narrow gorge formed by the surrounding hills, and rushes down a series of waterfalls with a total drop of 33 meters. For several hundreds of years, the streaming water had been used as a power source for flour mills and sawmills, but now, with the industrial development in the 19th century, an increasing number of factories crowded along the rapids to make use of their driving power. Most of them were located on the islands Önan and Malgön, which formed the first industrial center of Trollhättan. Soon there were paper mills, spinning factories as well as oil

Industries at Önan (in the foreground) and Malgön (further off to the left), early 20th century.[299]

101

works along the banks of the river. Trollhättan Mechanical Factories (Nohab), manufacturer of locomotives and later turbines for hydraulic power plants, was founded in 1847. In 1865, the first steam locomotive rolled out through the doors of the factory.

In 1800 a canal with locks was completed to allow ships to pass the waterfalls. One of the driving forces behind the building of the canal was Baltzar von Platen, older brother of the Baroness Charlotte Haij of Onsjö. For the first time, goods could now be transported all the way from Lake Vänern to the sea without trans-shipments. In order to further increase the capacity of the locks, a second branch was built in 1838-44 under the command of the famous canal builder Nils Ericsson.[6] Now more and larger vessels could pass, and Trollhättan's potential to grow as a center for industry and trade was further improved.

Population growth and periods of famine forced an ever-growing number of people to flee the countryside with the hope of finding a better life in urban areas. Adjacent to the saw mills, lodgings were built for the increasing number of workers, and when there was not enough space next to the factories, even more lodgments were erected on the outskirts of the community. One of those areas was Stavre Mosse, two and a half kilometers north-east of the rapids in Trollhättan. There, families lived in crowded quarters, plagued by poverty. Poor sanitary conditions led to recurring epidemics. In 1850, Trollhättan itself had about one thousand inhabitants with another 250 at Stavre Mosse.

When Jonas Eriksson moved to Trollhättan in 1837, he did not reveal his real place of birth to the pastor.[300] In the Catechetical Hearing Register of 1838, he is erroneously said to be born in the parish Ör in Dalsland.[301] The church of Ör is located 13 kilometers northwest of the church of Bolstad. The parishes did not even border to one another, but were separated by the parish

---

[6] To Amercians he is probably better known as the older brother of the inventor John Ericsson, constructor of the armored war ship USS Monitor.

of Erikstad. Still, we can be fairly certain that we are tracing the right Jonas Eriksson, since

- no Jonas Eriksson was born in Ör in 1812,

- through distinct page references, we can trace Jonas Eriksson backwards through register after register, until his birth in Bolstad in 1812 (with some uncertainty for the years 1821-23 due to missing pages in the Catechetical Hearing Register), and

- when Jonas married *Cajsa Andersdotter*, the names of the parents of the bridegroom as stated in the Marriage Register of Trollhättan, are identical to the names of Jonas' parents in the Birth Register of Bolstad.

What caused the error in the Hearing Register? Surely, in the second Catechetical Hearing, Jonas must have stated his place of birth himself, since it appears neither in the Relocation Register, nor in the first Catechetical Hearing Register. The pastor can hardly have misheard "Bolstad" for "Ör." Did Jonas himself believe that he was born in Ör? This is difficult to believe. Did he consciously report a fake birth place in an attempt to conceal his shameful background? We will never know for sure.

During his first years in Trollhättan, Jonas served at an inn. In 1839 he married a girl named Carolina Svensdotter,[302] and in the same year he moved from the inn to a rented lodgment at Stavre Mosse. There, the couple remained all of their life together.[303] Jonas had now found work at one of the saw mills.

Jonas and Carolina had five children:

- Edvard, born on June 6, 1840,[304]

- Johan Fredrik, born on April 13, 1842,[305]

- Charlotta, born on June 8, 1844,[306] dead from smallpox on May 4, 1852,[307]

- Carl, born on July 24, 1847,[308] and

- Johanna Sofia, born on May 13, 1850.[309]

Photo from Stavre Mosse 1929.[310]

In 1850, Trollhättan was hit by a cholera epidemic. The infection mainly spread in poor and over-populated districts. In October, eleven persons succumbed to the disease at Stavre Mosse. One of them was Carolina Svensdotter.[311] After her death, Jonas was left to tend to their five children on his own. At the time, they were between five months and ten years of age.[312] Two years later, his then seven-year-old daughter died in an epidemic of smallpox. The family remained at Stavre Mosse but moved between different lodgings. Jonas continued to work in the saw mill.[313] Considering the fact that there was no regulation of working hours in the 1850's, it is difficult to understand how he could possibly manage caring for his family in addition to the demands of his occupation. In 1856, for the first time, a parliamentary bill limiting the workday to 12 hours, was introduced. It was, however, rejected.[314] The 8-hour working day that we now take for granted was not introduced until 1919, but at that time people worked six days a week, not five as they do today! [315]

Six happy years

On January 15, 1858, Jonas Eriksson and *Cajsa Andersdotter* celebrated their wedding.[316] Already the previous fall, *Cajsa* and her children *Maria Christina*, 14 years old, and Johanna Sofia, 12 years old, had moved in with Jonas at Stavre Mosse.[317] Three of Jonas' children still lived at home: Johan Fredrik, 16, Carl, 11, and Johanna Sofia, 8 years old. It must have come as a relief for both parties, when Jonas and *Cajsa* joined together as a family. As a result of the union, *Cajsa* could change rolls, from being a dependent pauper to becoming the wife of a man with permanent employment and a home of his own. Jonas, on the other hand, had found someone who could take care of his children and tend to the household while he was at work. However, practical matters were not the only reason for them to get married. As elderly, *Cajsa* had said that she had had three men and that she had loved all three of them with equal affection. "Whom should I chose when I get to heaven?" she asked. Who the third man was, we do not know; maybe a teenage romance, maybe a soul mate in the autumn of her life.

Before Jonas and *Cajsa* were married, Jonas rented the home at Stavre Mosse. Around the time of their wedding, he succeeded in borrowing enough money to buy the house. The name of the property was Sågen (= Sawmill) 2 no. 16. In the Catechetical Hearing Register the word "tenant" is now crossed out and replaced by "property owner under Johan Staaf."[318] The family remained living in the same house, but was nonetheless listed on a new page in the Catechetical Hearing Register every year. This seems to have been the accepted way of updating the registers in Trollhättan.[319]

In 1861, *Cajsa's* oldest daughter *Maria Svensdotter*, with the second name Christina, moved to Gothenburg.[320] According to narratives passed on to later generations, she served as a maid in a "fine family". Her place of work was in the kitchen, where she learned how to cook for gentlefolk. Our family's traditional way of preparing rice porridge (two hours cooking time, adding a little milk at a time, stirring regularly) is said to have its origin in her experience from that time. After a little less than two years in Gothenburg, she returned to her mother and step-father in the house on Stavre Mosse.[321]

While *Maria* was gone, her little sister Johanna Sofia also left home.[322] At the age of 16, she was first employed as a maid on the farm Lockerud in Blåsut west of Vänersborg.[323] The following year she moved to the Lancaster School of Vänersborg, which was located on the western side of the street Edsgatan, just north of the market place. The school admitted boys six years of age and older. The curriculum included reading, writing and simple mathematics. The teaching method applied in Lancaster schools was called "mutual instruction," which basically meant that older pupils taught their younger schoolmates, under the supervision of a teacher. In this way, single teachers could manage large classes, with the consequence that the operational expenses for Lancaster schools could be kept very low. As a maid at the school, Johanna Sofia was not engaged in teaching, but rather handled tasks like cooking, cleaning, running errands etc.[324]

In 1864, after one year at the Lancaster school, Johanna Sofia moved to Gothenburg.[325] There, she probably worked in a dressmaker's workshop, since, when she returned to Vänersborg four years later,[326] she was employed as an assistant seamstress to the dressmaker Johanna Torbjörnsdotter.[327] Not more than six months later, she resigned to move to the capital of Norway, Christiania, which later changed its name to Oslo. In the Relocation Register she is given the title seamstress.[328] Why did Johanna Sofia suddenly move so far away? The answer is easy to guess: after only two months in the new country, she married a carpenter's apprentice, six years her senior, named Andreas Pettersson Norgren, born in Sundals-Ryr, Dalsland. The two probably met in Gothenburg and agreed to get married as soon as he had found permanent employment. Why he chose to work in Christiania instead of seeking employment in Sweden we do not know. On June 18, 1870, Johanna Sofia bore a son, who was given the name Axel Julius. The following year, the family moved back to Gothenburg, and in May of 1872, welcomed another son.[329] His name was Carl Frithiof. About a month later, the family returned to Christiania,[330] where they succeeded in acquiring an apartment on Smålensgatan 14, slightly more than one kilometer east of the Central Station. Andreas now worked as a carpenter, producing wooden models for L. Engebredsen's Mechanical Factories. Johanna Sofia may have worked as a

Johanna Sofia Svensdotter Norgren

seamstress, receiving customers in their home. In 1876, a third child was born to the family, the daughter Jenny Sofie. [331] Looking back, Johanna Sofia's success story surpassed the dreams of earlier generations. Although she was born to cottage dwellers in the countryside, lost her father before she turned four and had lived most of her youth as a dependent pauper, she succeeded in obtaining a professional education and in forming a well-established, middle class family in one of the national capitals of Scandinavia. On some occasions later in her life, she visited her sister in Trollhättan, and our grandmother Elin recounted that her aunt, with the slight Norwegian accent, was a "fine lady." Her photo confirms this impression.

Two empty hands

What happened to *Cajsa* and the rest of the family at Stavre Mosse when Johanna Sofia moved out? Unfortunately, the course of their lives was not at all as successful as hers. In the fall of 1864, the father of the family, Jonas Ericsson, fell sick. He had acquired a combination of pneumonia and hepatitis, and, after a short time in bed, he passed away, only 52 years old.[332] Sadly, *Cajsa* and Jonas were only able to enjoy six years together.

Jonas' death necessitated a rather complicated estate distribution. The estate inventory, which can be found complete among the supplements, gives the impression of certain prosperity. *Cajsa*, who was used to the poverty of a dependent tenant, must have thought it a luxury to have a complete set of cooking utensils, kitchen tools, furniture, and clothes among her possessions, not to mention two paintings and a wall clock! And in spite of the crowding at Stavre Mosse, they even had room for a "swine animal" of their own. The house and the private property were evaluated to 255 riksdaler, but when the inventory was completed, it turned out that Jonas was also 148 riksdaler in debt, mainly to three private persons. It must have been from them that Jonas had borrowed the funds to buy the house. Now his family was forced to sell the home in order to pay his debts. The buyer was a man named Johannes Lundberg.[333] Unfortunately, the estate inventory holds no information on the division of the inheritance, but we can assume this is what happened:

At the time of the death of Jonas Ericsson, estate distributions were still regulated by the National Law of 1734, with the exception that equal inheritance rights for men and women had been introduced in 1845. The result of this change was that the surviving spouse, independent of sex, was assigned half of the value of the estate as marital property, and that sons and daughters inherited equal shares.[334] Out of the 107 riksdaler that remained when the debts were paid, *Cajsa* at the most received 1/20 as her favored article, 1/10 as her morning gift and 1/2 as her marital property, which adds up to, at the most, 70 riksdaler. The remaining 37 riksdaler must have been divided equally among Jonas' four remaining children. The two oldest, his sons Edvard and Johan Fredrik, now lived in Stockholm. They probably received 9 riksdaler each, along with their two younger siblings. One detail worth mentioning is that *Cajsa*, to ensure that the estate was correctly and honestly declared, signed her name "with hand on pen". This means that she held on to the pen, while one of the inventory executors wrote her name. We already know that *Cajsa* had earned the grade "well" for reading, but obviously she had never mastered the skill of writing.

Now, four inhabitants remained in the house at Stavre Mosse: *Cajsa*, *Maria* and Jonas' two youngest children Carl and Johanna Sofia (not to be confused with *Cajsa's* daughter Johanna Sofia who at this time lived in Gothenburg). It must have been sad to live as tenants in a house that, just a few months earlier, had been their own. Jonas' children did not remain there for long. In 1865, Carl moved to Trökörna outside of Grästorp to work as a farmhand.[335] The following year, Johanna Sofia moved to Vänersborg, where she had found employment as a maid.[336] Now *Cajsa* and *Maria* were the only remaining occupants in the house. In the Catechetical Hearing Register, *Cajsa* is said to be "sickly, not fit for work". Her inherited 70 riksdaler were soon spent on food and rent. Already the same year, they were forced to leave the house in Stavre Mosse to move to Hebe no. 1 in Trollhättan. Undoubtedly, this was not a joyful transition, since Hebe no. 1 was Trollhättan's poorhouse.

Chapter 7:

Cajsa Andersdotter in Trollhättan

In the poorhouse

Cajsa's experience in Trollhättan began with her move to the poorhouse. She was now 48 years old and was already twice a widow. Her oldest daughter *Maria*, age 22, moved in with her.[337] The ground floor of the poor house was divided into four single rooms, each housing one family. A few additional rooms were located on the first floor. The paupers cooked most of their food in a collective kitchen. According to what *Cajsa* later recounted, the food mostly consisted of watery porridge made of ground rye, oats or peas, dry pieces of bread, and sometimes a chunk of cheese or a slice of sausage. The paupers received money for buying the ingredients from doles and church offerings, but they also had to contribute themselves according to their ability. For example, they could spin thread from flax or wool. It is possible that *Cajsa* was able to manufacture hats on demand, since there is a saying in the family that she was "Trollhättan's first milliner." Perhaps she had learned to make hats during her year at Onsjö?

In 1868-70, Sweden was again struck by severe crop failure. Lack of food made prices soar. In the poorhouse, the paupers received extra support,[338] but herring sperm was the only meat available. In the countryside, packs of starving beggars wandered from village to village. Many poor provincials found their way to the cities, hoping to find work. Others auctioned away all their belongings to buy a ticket to America. It was not unusual that the breadwinner in the family had perished in a work accident, since the concept of industrial safety was still unknown. In 1875, an extension was added to the poorhouse at Hebe no. 1 in order to make room for more penniless paupers.[339]

In Trollhättan, the pastors made separate lists of paupers in the Catechetical Hearing Registers. For some of the tenants, they noted various traits or disabilities like "fool," "naïve," "almost blind" or "lame." For others, they registered nicknames like "Beata in the stand," "Goose," "Haddock" or "Crook-leg." In all of the registers from 1871 to 1902, *Cajsa* was nicknamed "Glädje" (= Joy) or "Glädje-Cajsa."[340] In all probability, this name originated from her first husband's name, *Sven Andersson Glädje*. Perhaps she was called Glädje-Cajsa as a distinguishing byname, during the time she was living with him at Malöga? The name apparently followed her to Stavred Mosse and, finally, to the poor house in Trollhättan, where it was likely understood as a nickname. People who were unaware of the origin of the name must have associated it with words like "gläjdehus" (= "joy house" = whore house) and "glädjeflicka" (= "joy girl" = prostitute). Thirty years later, when *Cajsa* moved to her daughter's family and was no longer classified as a pauper, the pastor immediately stopped adding the nickname to her name in the Hearing Registers.[341] Obviously, it was only to paupers that the pastors were not obliged to show respect. However, "Glädjen" (= The joy) later turned up again as a nickname for *Cajsa's* oldest grandchild. Another example of the same disrespect was that all paupers in Trollhättan were given the grade c for reading as well as for reciting Luther's Catechism and explanations.[342] It is quite possible that the pastor had not even bothered to listen to them, since we know from previous records concerning her capabilities that *Cajsa* was skilled in all three areas.

A savior in times of need

In late spring of 1868, after less than two years at the poorhouse, it was evident that *Cajsa's* daughter *Maria* was expecting a baby. Giving birth without being married was a disgrace, but fortunately *Maria* was spared this humiliation. On June 28, a shoemaker named *Johannes Svensson* from Vänersborg had the banns published to marry her, and on August 2, they celebrated their wedding.[343] It took a couple of months for the young couple to find a home of their own. As a result, on September 9,

1868, their first child, a son named Frithiof Julius, was born in Trollhättan's poorhouse.[344]

Who was the shoemaker *Johannes Svensson*? He was born on December 2, 1839, in the Parish of Ödsmål in Bohuslän, immediately north of what is today known as the town of Stenungsund.[7] His mother, *Marta Berntsdotter* (1815-69), was not married, but in the Birth Register the father of the child is said to be the cottager's son *Sven Torkelsson* from Byn.[345] *Marta* had already worked as a maid in Ödsmål[346] and the neighbor parishes of Ucklum[347] and Norum,[348] when she, at the age of 24, must have realized that she was expecting a baby. She continued to work until the end of the employment year and then moved back to her parents' hill cottage at Rågårdsmyren under Bua.[349] Three of her seven siblings still lived at home, so when *Johannes* was born, he found himself sharing what was probably the only room of the cottage with his mother, his grandmother, his grandfather, two uncles and one aunt.[350] During the years 1809-21, his grandfather, *Bernt Thoresson* (1784-1854), had served in Bohuslän Second Navy Seaman Company, where he had been given the soldier's name Frimodig (= Fearless).[351] After his dismissal from the navy, he lived as a pauper and hill cottage dweller. By the way, he was not the only military man in the family. His father-in-law, *Bernt Andersson* (1743-1813), had also served as a navy seaman under the soldier's name Krabbe.[352]

Over the years, *Marta's* siblings found employment as farmhands and maids in the area, with the result that there was eventually more room in the hill cottage. When *Johannes* turned nine, his mother finally also moved out, but not to serve as a maid. Instead, she had accepted a marriage proposal from a painter and cottager ten years her junior, named Carl P. Elfström[353] and moved in with him in the cottage Banken under Pjökeröd in the same parish.[354] According to traditions in the family, in her youth, *Martha* was called "black Martha" because of her pitch

---

[7] This birth date can be found in the Birth- and Baptism Register. In all later registers, *Johannes* is erroneously said to born on December 22, 1839.

black hair. After marrying a painter, her distinguishing byname changed to "Painter's Martha". She now bore three children:

- Julia, born on March 24, 1850,[355] died on April 18, 1855,[356]
- Augustinus, born on January 6, 1853,[357] and
- Bernhard, born on October 1, 1857.[358]

Marta did not invite *Johannes* to join her when she moved in with her new husband. Instead, he stayed with his grandparents in the hill cottage at Rågårdsmyren. It was located next to Lake Hällungen, which *Johannes*, later in life, thinking of his child-hood, called "my lake." When his grandparents became too old to manage on their own, they left the hill cottage to live with their son, the cottager Christian Berntsson at Grinden under Bräcke. *Johannes* moved with them.[359] In 1854 his grandfather died.[360] *Johannes*, who was now old enough to start working, like most other young men in the countryside, sought employ-ment as a farmhand.[361] After just one year of work for an em-ployer outside the family, he decided to move to live with his mother and step-father at Banken under Pjökeröd. Here, he is first called a farmhand, then a dependant tenant, then a lay about[8] and finally "Marta's son".[362] A possible interpretation is that his step-father first hired him (farmhand), then demanded economic compensation from the parish for housing him (de-pendant tenant), and finally persuaded him to work without a formal employment contract and with room and board as his only compensation (lay about, Marta's son)? Under these condi-tions, *Johannes* lived for ten years until finally, at the age of 27, he decided to try something else. On October 17, 1867, he vis-ited the parish office to report his intention to move out. When the pastor asked his profession, he answered "worker". And where was he moving? To Vänersborg, forty kilometers away from his home parish.[363]

Here we run into an unexpected problem in our attempt to map *Johannes'* life. In Vänersborg's Relocation Register for 1867, there is no *Johannes Svensson* moving in from Ödsmål. The

---

[8] "Lay about" was up to 1885 a term for unemployed.

same is true for the Relocation Register of Vassända-Naglum, sometimes called Vänersborg Country Parish. For the Catechetical Hearing Registers of Vänersborg, an alphabetical name register has been created, but even there we cannot find *Johannes Svensson* from Ödsmål. The following year, he married *Maria Svensdotter* and moved to Trollhättan, where the Relocation Register states that he moved in from Vänersborg on November 10.[364] However, he is neither found listed among the inhabitants moving out from Vänersborg nor from Vassända-Naglum. Could he have lived somewhere else during 1867-68? This is hardly probable, for in Trollhättan's Marriage Register is noted that he "presented Certificate of No Impediment to Marriage from Vänersborg".

Another astonishing fact is that *Johannes*, who until 1867 never had any other profession than farmhand or worker, not more than one year later, is called shoemaker in the registers of Trollhättan. Did this title not require an extensive, professional education? Ever since the Middle Ages, those who wanted to become craftsmen within a guild, first had to train as an apprentice, then as a journeyman, and, finally, pass a test to become a master. This process required several years, but with the breakthrough of industrialism and the migration to the cities, the old way of organizing craftsmen in guilds became outdated. In 1846, Parliament passed a bill softening the guild system, and in 1864 it was finally abolished. Now, anyone who regarded himself as having the ability, could call himself a shoemaker, a tailor, a carpenter, etc.

A question which remains unanswered is how *Johannes* and *Maria* met. It is likely that he worked for a shoemaker in Vänersborg, while she was residing at Trollhättan's poorhouse. If *Johannes* was the father of *Maria's* first child, they must have met very soon after his transition to Vänersborg, since he left Ödsmål no earlier than October 17, 1867, and *Maria* became pregnant in December of the same year. However, fate often finds surprising pathways. Maybe *Johannes'* employer in Vänersborg sent him to sell shoes at some market in Trollhättan during the late fall of 1867?

The industrious shoemaker

On November 10, 1868, *Maria* and her two-month-old son, Julius, left the poorhouse for good. It must have been a great relief for her when she, together with *Johannes* and their child, could move into a rented apartment on the block Trollet (= the troll). Later, the family moved a number of times, before *Johannes*, in 1872, finally managed to buy a house at Diana 4, which became their permanent home.

There may have been different reasons for their many moves. In all likelihood, *Johannes'* shoemaking business attracted an increasing number of customers, which forced him to find a larger workshop. Another reason may have been the continuous growth of the family which required more space. Below is the list of Johannes' and Maria's children (the name underlined is the name used to address the person):

- Frithiof <u>Julius</u>, born on September 9, 1868,[365] died on October 23, 1953,
- <u>Ivar</u> Ferdinand, born on January 21, 1870,[366] died on September 21, 1959,
- Gustaf <u>Henning</u>, born on March 2, 1871,[367] died on April 24, 1956,
- Amalia Sofia ("Mali"), born on October 8, 1872,[368] died on December 19, 1962,
- Karl Mattvig, born on November 22, 1873,[369] died in diphtheria on September 14, 1876,[370]
- Johan <u>Albin</u>, born on April 1, 1875,[371] died on December 20, 1956,
- Karl <u>Hilding</u>, born on January 8, 1879,[372] died on June 30, 1970,
- Sven Fingal ("<u>Alan</u>"), born on June 30, 1880,[373] died on November 1, 1953,

115

- Johannes Emanuel ("Jonnar"), born on November 13, 1881,[374] died on August 23, 1968,

- Karl Anders Engelbrekt, born on November 14, 1883,[375] died in "convulsiones" on March 3, 1886,[376]

- Jenny Emilia ("Meli"), born on May 21, 1885,[377] died on April 5, 1979,

- *Elin Viktoria*, born on February 20, 1888,[378] died on December 29, 1969, and

- Hilma Fredrika, born on January 28, 1890,[379] died on January 27 1965.

How could *Johannes* afford buying a house of his own, when he had only managed his shoemaker's business for five years and already had several children to feed? One explanation could be that Diana 4 was located on "unfree ground", which most probably lowered the price. This meant that the property owner only possessed the very buildings, not the ground on which they were located. For the ground, he had to pay an annual leaseholder's rent to the municipality. Furthermore, there was probably only one rather small one-and-a-half story building on the lot when *Johannes* bought the property. It simply had to suffice, both as a shoemaker's workshop and as a home for the family, but neither he nor *Maria* had been spoiled with any luxury earlier in life. Like the rest of the children in the family, our grandmother *Elin* grew up in the small house, which she called "the house on the hill", since it was located on a small, barren stone hill. Later, *Johannes* had a larger building erected next to the street, but his family never moved there. Instead, he rented it out to secure their financial situation. Today, neither the buildings, nor the hill itself remain at Diana 4. They have been replaced by modern development. Among the historical maps of the Land Surveying Authority, there is a map of Trollhättan from 1893. There, both the smaller house in the interior of the lot ("the house on the hill"), and the larger building, located along the street Österlång-gatan ("the house by the street") are visible, as well as a shared shed for firewood and tools (see map).

Towards the end of the 19th century, cameras were more generally introduced. The Innovatum Photo Archive holds many photos from early Trollhättan, but it is difficult to find any photos from Diana 4. In 1907, a photo of the central part of town was taken from the newly erected water tower on the block Skottön. In the foreground we can see what was later to become the Queen's Market, and further to the back, the block Diana. Looking closely, one can distinguish both parts of the house by the street, the house on the hill and the shared shed (see photo).

Now that we have come to that period of time, which our grandmother *Elin* herself had experienced, more first-hand stories are preserved concerning the different members of the family. According to *Elin*, her mother *Maria* was strict and firm. She ordered her children to work, much like she had probably been ordered herself as a child, after she had lost her father, and the family lived as tenant paupers at Malöga. *Elin*, who in her teens sometimes suffered from frailness, used to sneak away to the neighbors to rest for a while. Her grandmother, *Cajsa*, periodically came from the poorhouse to visit them, and *Elin* enjoyed her company.

Ever since the middle ages, there was a tradition in Sweden that women, after each child birth, should undergo a so-called churching. It prescribed that they must refrain from going to church for six weeks, while their bodies recovered and were "purified." When this period was over, they were re-introduced to the congregation with a special ceremony. This tradition continued during all of the 19th century, but *Maria* never attended a churching, despite the fact that she bore 13 children. She excused herself by claiming that she did not have nice enough clothes. One cannot, however, rule out the possibility that the growing labor movement's resistance to the church influenced her decision.

Elin's father *Johannes* was in several respects the opposite of his wife. He was mild-tempered and understanding, and always intervened when his wife threatened to hit the children. He often tried to sooth her by calling her "my heart" or "my little dove". Also, he engaged himself socially for peace and justice. Politi-

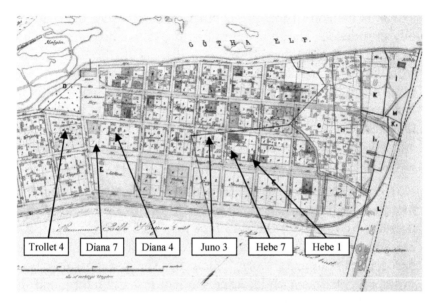

Detail of map of Trollhättan, dated 1893, showing locations where *Cajsa's* daughter *Maria* lived between 1866 and 1918 (the year of her death):

Hebe 1 (poorhouse) 1866-68
Juno 3 .... 1869-70 [381]
Diana 7 .... 1871-72 [383]

Trollet 4 .... 1868-69 [380]
Hebe 7 .... 1870-71 [382]
Diana 4 .... 1872-1918 [384]

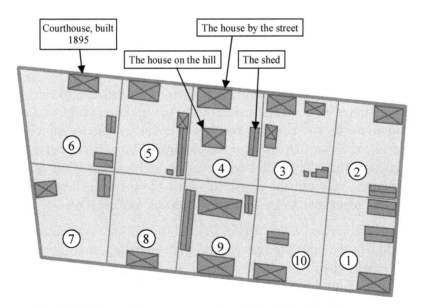

The block Diana with property numbers. Detail from the above map.

The shed

The house on the hill

The house by the street

The courthouse

Detail from photo made from the new water tower in the block Skottön 1909. Innovatums Photo Archive, no. ISC-2004-053.

The shoemaker *Johannes Svensson* and his wife *Maria Svensdotter*.

cally, he sympathized with the labor movement, and on the defense question, his stance was clear as glass: No one has the right to take another person's life, so logically, war is always wrong! With deep commitment he taught his children to pay attention when walking to avoid stepping on ants. The rats, which made their way into his shoemaker's workshop to gnaw on the leather, he caught alive in a trap-like cage. Every morning he carried the cage out and let the rats go. *Elin* claimed that she recognized every single rat, since they soon learned to find their way straight back to the workshop.

As soon as the sons reached their teens, they volunteered to help their father in the workshop, and since neither gramophone nor radio were yet at hand, they sang while hob nailing shoes. In those days, poems from the cycle *The Tales of Ensign Stål* by Johan Ludvig Runeberg, set to music, were popular. *Johannes*, however, who was otherwise so mild and understanding, strictly forbade his sons to sing them. He could not endure listening to how Runeberg glorified war in poems like *The soldier boy*:[9]

> *And if I live till I am big and reach fifteen some day,*
> *to that same hunger, war and death, I go without dismay.*
> *When whizzing bullets fill the air,*
> *whoever seeks me, finds me there,*
> *for I, in turn, will follow where*
> *my fathers led the way.*

It is not an elementary task to calculate how many people lived in the house on the hill from year to year. In 1888 the oldest son Julius enrolled in the Second Company of the Royal Göta Artillery Regiment in Karlsborg.[385] A natural guess is that he did so as a protest against his father's pacifism. Two years later, he returned home, and, after he had married, both he and his wife moved into the house on the hill. There they had a son, before they, in 1892, moved to a home of their own by the paper mill, where Julius was now employed as a worker.[386] In the same year, the son Henning married. He and his wife also moved in with the family. The following year, it was Ivar's turn to get married, but, in contrast to the others, he and his wife found a home of their own from the very beginning. On the other hand, Henning's family remained in the house on the hill until they had two sons, before they finally moved to Gothenburg in

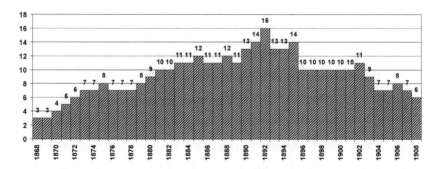

Number of family members in *Johannes'* and *Maria's*
household during the period 1868-1908.

---

[9] Translation by Charles Wharton Stork.

1896.[387] Henning was very interested in the new photography techniques and later in life became a reputable photographer.

The movement of people in and out of the house on the hill was not limited to family members. *Johannes'* shoemaking business flourished, and soon he could no longer depend on his sons' temporary support. In 1888, a shoemaker by the name of Karl August Selander moved in with the family.[388] He remained there for the rest of his life and was probably regarded as a family member. In all likelihood, *Johannes* met Selander during his year in Vänersborg, where they both trained to be shoemakers. Despite the fact that Selander was eleven years younger than *Johannes*, they shared several tragic, common experiences: both were born out of wedlock, both had mothers who had left them, but while *Johannes* lived with his grandparents as a child, Selander had grown up in Vänersborg's poorhouse. He walked with a limp, and even at an adult age he depended on support from the municipality.[389] Maybe this was one of the reasons the warm-hearted *Johannes* chose to employ him rather than someone else.

Now that several of *Johannes'* and *Maria's* children had moved out, the financial situation of the family gradually strengthened due to the income, not only from the shoemaking business, but also from the rent from the house by the street. Finally, another move became possible. During a span of thirty years, grandmother *Cajsa* had lived in Trollhättan's poorhouse,[390] but now she spent the last phase of her life in the house on the hill. It is difficult to determine the exact date of her move there, since in the Congregation Registers, which in 1895 replaced the Catechetical Hearing Registers, she is still listed under paupers, but with an additonal comment: "Diana 4, no support". This probably indicates that she had already left the poorhouse.[391] By the year 1902, when she had reached 84 years of age, she definitely lived with her family. She had her own room on the upper floor of the house, which must have felt like an enormous improvement, compared to the cottages and the poorhouse where she had spent almost all of her life. Her granddaughter *Elin* spent much time with her. This must have given *Cajsa* the opportunity to tell the story of her life, from serving the king a glass of water to seeing her husband and father-in-law drown. Sometimes, *Elin's* mother *Maria* would come up the stairs to tell them to do something more productive than just sitting around chatting. She was used to being the one who ruled over the household. Then *Cajsa* would burst out: "Maria! Who is the mother of whom? Am I the mother of you, or are you the mother of me?"

The family, which had been large and overcrowded, now had more space with every child that left the house. Meli moved to Gothenburg in 1902.[392] Hilding married and moved to a home of his own in Trollhättan in 1903. Mali and Jonnar did likewise in 1904. On the other hand, Albin's wife moved in with the family, where she bore a daughter in 1906.[393] Later the same year, Hilma moved to Gothenburg.[394]

It was, however, not only the moving out of the children that reduced the size of the family. When *Johannes* turned 60 his health began to falter. He had recurring headaches and finally was confined to bed. One may expect that he would complain about his pain, but he never did. On the contrary, he said with a smile that he had never had a better life. By this time, he did not have to work, and food was served to him by his bedside, as if he were royalty. His condition gradually worsened, and he eventually became both lame and blind. On June 2, 1903, he finally passed away. The underlying cause of his death was attributed to a brain tumor.[395]

In the Estate Inventory conducted after *Johannes* death, it appears that he owned all of the buildings on the lot Diana 4, as well as all household effects (see supplement). Aside from the ordinary household accessories and the shoemaker's tools, the house on the hill held one luxury article: an American wall clock. We do not know where it might have hung. Perhaps it was placed in the workshop to impress customers? Another interesting detail is the fact that, aside from six chairs, the house held *five* old wooden settles. Most likely they were daybeds where the

Photo from Karl August Selander's funeral on September 20, 1908. Maria (no. 8) och eight of her eleven child appear in the photo. Most probably Henning stood behind the camera. Albin and Meli are missing.

children had slept two by two, or when the family was most numerous, three by three. It is also worth noting that *Johannes* had no debts at all. From the time he left Ödsmål with two empty hands in 1867, he had until his death, through hard work, succeeded in acquiring a house of his own and a building he could lease, all the while supporting a family with eleven children, and, during his last years, also supporting his impoverished mother-in-law. For his surviving family, he had created a basic but stable financial situation. His widow *Maria* remained living in the house on the hill until she died in 1918. She never had to return to the poorhouse again.

On September 20, 1907, *Cajsa* passed away peacefully. She was then 89 years old and still mentally alert and lucid. The cause of death is said to be "old age fading".[396] The following year, Johannes' shoemaker colleague Selander also passed away. After many years, friends had helped him buy a train ticket to Stockholm to visit his mother. Maybe this experience was too overwhelming, since on the journey back home, he had a stroke and died shortly after arriving in Trollhättan.[397] Most of the family members as well as friends and neighbors attended his funeral. The enclosed photo from this unique occasion is taken "on the hill" with the house by the street in the background. Chances are good that the man behind the camera was Henning, who at the time worked as a professional photographer in Gothenburg.

Names and fatherhood

We have now reached the end of the story about *Cajsa Andersdotter*. Through her daughter *Maria*, *Cajsa* had 11 grandchildren, 40 great-grandchildren, 36 great-great-grandchildren, and 61 great-great-great-grandchildren. Two of her grandchildren emigrated to America. How many descendants *Cajsa* had through her daughter Johanna Sofia, who moved to Norway, we do not know.

Those of my readers, who have taken the pains to go through the estate inventory after *Johannes Svensson* in the supplement, may have noticed that his children used different last names when signing the document. This may seem odd, but like most human phenomena it has an historical explanation.

Within the Swedish nobility, family names appeared already in the Middle Ages, while commoners generally were called by their first name followed by their father's first name with the addition -son or -dotter (= daughter). In the 16th century, many clergymen began to create family names for themselves, often Latinized forms of some geographical name from their home area, such as Helsingus, Angermannus, or Elfdalius. Soldiers were given distinguishing names related to their character like Glad, Tapper (= Courageous), or Frimodig (= Fearless). In time, these names were used as family names by their descendants. Toward the end of the 19th century, it became increasingly popular for common people to create family names for themselves and for their immediate families, often with associations to some place, lake, plant etc. In 1901, a bylaw was passed stating that all Swedes must have a family name, which would then be inherited from parents to children. Those who had not selected a family name by 1904 would be given their father's first name with the addition -son as family name. This referred to both men and women. Until this date, with few restrictions, it was possible to freely select your family name. [398]

Cajsa's last name serves as a good example of how family names developed in Sweden. In 1818, when she was born, she was called Greta Cajsa Andersdotter, since her father's first name was Anders. She kept the name Andersdotter even after marrying *Sven Andersson* in 1842 and Jonas Eriksson in 1858. In the estate inventory following Jonas' death in 1865, the executor calls her Kajsa Andersson. Obviously, women still refrained from adopting the last name of their husband, but the custom of replacing -dotter with -son in women's last name was already introduced. Twenty years later, in Trollhättan Catechetical Hearing Register of 1884-90, the pastor starts calling her by her late husband's last name, but still prefers ending it in -doter (dialect for dotter = daughter) rather than -son, "Kajsa Ereksdoter".[399]

This last name stays with her until 1902. After her move from the poorhouse to her daughter's family at Diana 4, she is still first called Kajsa Eriksdotter, but this is later changed to Kajsa Eriksson. There is also a note in the register that she was born Landgren.[400]

In order to meet the legal requirement to adopt a family name no later then 1904, *Maria's* children selected different names:

- Julius called himself Fridén,
- Ivar, Henning, and Albin called themselves Landgren,
- Hilding, Alan, and Hilma called themselves Svensson Landgren,
- Jonnar called himself Johansson,
- Mali received her husband's name Forsberg,
- Meli received her husband's name Fransson, and
- Elin received her husband's name Nyman.

A natural guess is that Julius choose his family name because of its association with words like "fri" (= free) and "frihet" (= freedom). All of his life, he was said to have difficulties yielding to authorities. Naturally, those who called themselves Landgren had taken the name of their great-grandfather, *Anders Olsson Landgren*. Some of them have also added their father's last name, Svensson. Jonnar probably called himself Johansson after his father's first name Johannes following the tradition that common people had applied for centuries. Maybe this was his way of protesting against his siblings' more pretentious way of creating family names. The fact that Mali, Meli and Elin adopted their husband's family names was simply in accordance with the new bylaw.

Six of the siblings, thus, adopted the name Landgren. Soon, a myth about the origin of the name started to circulate within the family. Their forefather *Anders Olsson* was said to have been called to a man abiding death. Earlier in life he had been a rich farmer, but fate had bereaved him of both house and land. Now he was lying on his deathbed, and when *Anders* entered the room he said: "I have lost all my belongings, and therefore I have only one thing to give to you. You shall bear my name, Landgren, because I am your father." From that day on, Anders Olsson took on the family name Landgren.

I have made much effort to prove the truth of this story without success. Among other attempts, I have examined not only the Death and Funeral Registers of Gestad, where Anders was born and lived all of his life, but also the equivalent registers of the neighbor parishes Bolstad, Grinstad and Erikstad. I have searched these registers from 1841, which is the last year possible for the pastor to have made the note that *Anders* called himself Landgren, and twenty years backwards in time, without finding any person named Landgren. I have also searched other registers without finding any Landgren in the area around Gestad during the relevant period. Therefore, my conclusion is that the story most probably is made up, and that *Anders* simply chose the name himself. In the mid 19th century, it was becoming a custom to adopt family names, and for a man who had lived all of his life in the country, Landgren may have seemed a natural choice (land = country, gren = branch). It also appears quite understandable that his great-grandchildren, who were the off-spring of paupers on both their father's and their mother's side, felt a need to improve the status of their family name.

The tale about the origin of the name Landgren was not the only myth that flourished in the family. As I have already mentioned, the siblings' father, *Johannes*, was an illegitimate child. It did not take long before he was presented as the son of a nobleman. His mother *Marta* was said to have served under a Baronet Hvit-fedt, whose son fell in love her and made her pregnant. The baronet then intervened and persuaded a farmhand named Sven to marry her. This was supposed to be how *Johannes* acquired his last name Svensson. A story like this is easy to refute. When *Marta* became pregnant, she worked as a maid for the farmer Sven Hansson and his wife Anna Christina Johnsdotter at Näb-begrind under Stenung Nedergården in Norum Parish.[401] Just a few kilometers away lay Byn Sörgården in Ödsmål Parish, where Sven Torkelsson lived, the man who according to the Birth Register was *Johannes'* father. Maybe his name and position inspired the part of the story about the farmhand named Sven? However, as I have mentioned earlier in this chapter, Sven never married *Marta*. According to the church registers, there was no Baronet Hvitfedt, neither in Ödsmål nor in the neighboring parishes.

It was not only for their own family that the siblings on the hill made up stories in order to create more status. *Johannes* colleague and tenant, the disabled Karl August Selander, was also an illegitimate child. Who could have been his father? Soon the suggestion circulated in the family that he was the son of the famous English bear hunter and author Llewellyn Lloyd (1792-1876). At the time that Selander was conceived, in 1849, Lloyd rented a room at Gäddebäck under Onsjö, which was still under the rule of the General's Wife Charlotte Haij. At the same time, Selander's mother, Sofia Niklasdotter, worked as a maid in the cottage Sinaiberg under Onsjö on the other side of the river Göta Älv. Theoretically, they might have met. The fact that she was 23 and he was 57 does not necessarily make the claimed fatherhood impossible. However, I leave it to the reader to judge weather Selander was likely the son of Lloyd or not.

What happened then?

The history of *Cajsa Andersdotter* and her family illustrates how poor people lived from the late 18th century to the early 20th century. Starvation, disease and child mortality constitute essential parts of the story, but *Cajsa's* fate also demonstrates how difficult it was for common people to move from a lower position to a higher position in society. Now, more than a hundred years later, much of the social structure has changed. *Cajsa's* great-great-grandchildren are no longer farmhands, maids, cottage dwellers or dependent tenants. On the contrary, they are teachers, engineers, dentists or economists. How was this possible?

Peace

Wars, which had been the cause of Sweden's economic ruin in the 17th and 18th century, came to an end in 1814. The country's resources could now be funneled into peaceful development. Non-alignment policy made it possible for Sweden to avoid being involved in either of the two World Wars. In 1945, at the end of World War II, great portions of Europe lay in ruins, while Sweden was intact. Soon, Swedish industry soared, delivering all kinds of products for the restoration of devastated countries. As a result, in the 1970's, Sweden was said to have the second highest standard of living in the world, surpassed only by the USA. Later, other developed countries caught up. Some have even taken the lead.

Industrial society

The population growth, which had caused severe problems during the 18th and 19th century, continued in the 20th. The mechanization of agricultural production generated an extreme reduction in the need for labor in the countryside. On the other hand, the growing modernization of industry required more workers. This encouraged a significant portion of the population to move from rural areas to the cities. Furthermore, between 1850 and 1920, 1.2 million Swedes immigrated to America. When the sale of contraceptives was made legal in 1938, the number of children per family drastically decreased. This sudden turn in nativity, in combination with the acute shortage of labor after World War II, resulted in extensive immigration, but also in another important change. Before this time, most women worked without compensation in their homes as so-called housewives. Between 1960 and 1985 daycare centers, run by the municipalities, were established for all children, and almost all women were able to find positions of paid employment. This soon proved to be a decisive step toward equality between the sexes. It also led to considerable improvements in the standard of living. In the past, most families lived on one income; now they had the possibility of benefiting from two. Having a car and a TV became matters of course, and the standard space for living quarters increased gradually. In the early 20th century, most families were crowded into one room and a kitchen. Today, the average floor surface in Sweden is 42 square meters per person. After 1980, economic liberalism and globalization have led to greater competition. Many traditionally Swedish companies have been taken over by international owners.

Sweden's population from 1750 to 2000

1750	1.8 millions
1800	2.4 millions
1850	3.5 millions
1900	5.1 millions
1950	7.0 millions
2000	8.9 millions

Social reform

The social security system that Swedes enjoy today was un-thinkable in the 19th century. Then, many of the elderly members of the population that could not support themselves were forced to live as dependent tenants or reside in over-crowded poor-houses. The old age pension, which was first introduced in 1913, was originally very modest. Working hours were not regulated until 1919, when a maximum of 48 hours per week was estab-lished. Since universal suffrage had been introduced in 1921, the labor movement gained increasing influence. During the period of 1936 to 1976, Sweden had social-democrat governments, and a number of social security reforms were introduced. After 1976, liberal/conservative and social-democrat governments have al-ternated. Differences in income, which shrank to a minimum in the 1980's, have since increased. Citizens without professional or university education, such as many refugee immigrants, now face difficulties finding reasonably paid jobs.

Examples of social security reforms introduced during the 20th century

1930	Maternity allowance
1935	Housing benefit for families with children
1938	Two weeks' vacation

1938	Public dental care
1948	Universal child support
1954	Motherhood insurance
1955	General health insurance
1963	Four weeks' vacation
1974	Parental insurance
1978	Five weeks' vacation

School

The four years of compulsory school, introduced in 1842, gradually increased to nine. This resulted in drastically improved possibilities for children of poor families to find employment. Today, 76 % of the Swedish population graduate from high school and are thus qualified for university studies. In 1992, the non-socialist government opened up for private companies to start schools, and gave all families the right to choose which school their children should attend, while still being fully financed by the municipality. This led to an increase in diversity, but also to growing social segregation between schools.

Number of compulsory years at school

1842	4
1882	6
1936	7
1950	8
1972	9

Since 1965, government financed loans are offered to all Swedes who decide to study on university level. Consequently, the parents' income is no longer a critical factor when choosing between work and higher studies. Today, 25 % of the population has studied at least three years on university level. Of those who graduate from university, 65 % are women.

Supplements

Kings/Queens and wars in Sweden 1600-2000

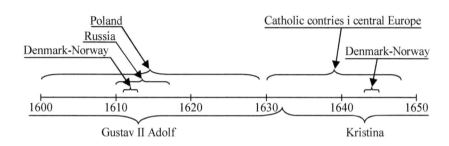

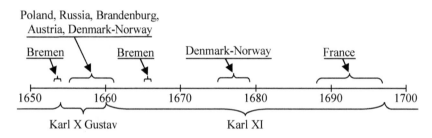

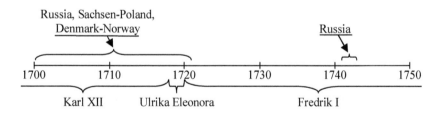

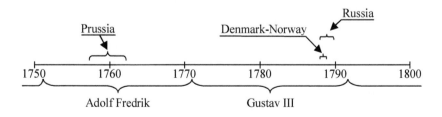

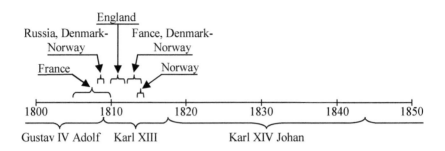

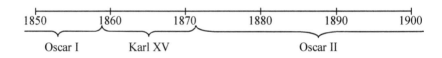

Historical maps of Sweden 1600-2000

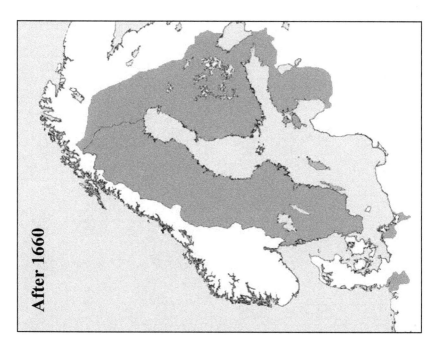

After 1660

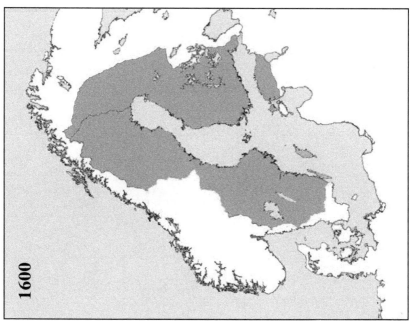

1600

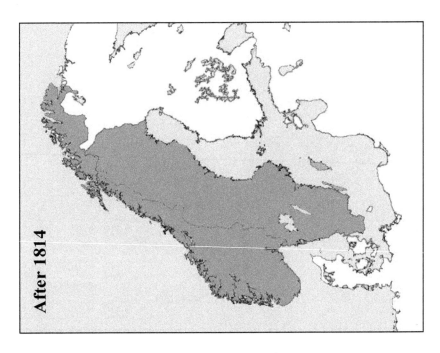

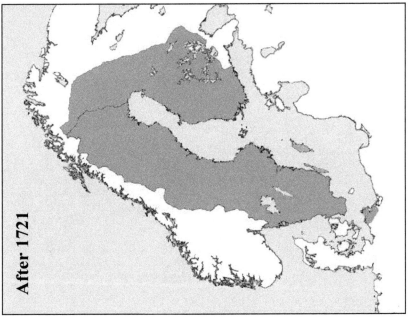

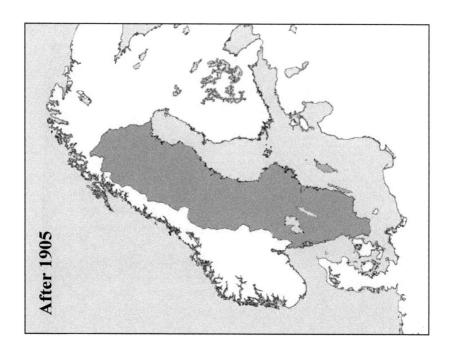

Estate inventory after Olof Jonsson (1745-1798) [402]

(Read more about this inventory on page 42)

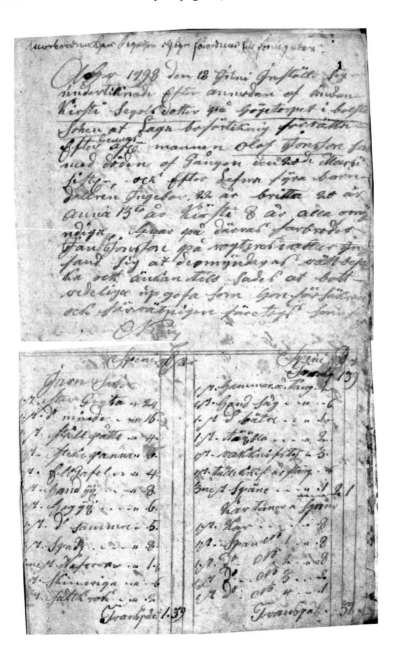

English translation

The Uncle Lars Segolsson in Höga appointed as trustee.

On June 12, 1798, the undersigned [executors] *appeared, after request from the widow Kirsti Segolsdotter at Högetorp in Bolstad Parish, in order to perform legal estate inventory after her deceased husband, Olof Jonsson, who gave in to death last March 20,[10] having four surviving children – the daughter Ingebor 22 years, Britta 20 years, Anna 13 years, and Kirsti 8 years, all under age.[11] Their uncle Jan Jonsson from Rågtvets Vallar appeared, in order to guard the rights of the under age* [daughters], *and the widow was instructed to declare the estate honestly which she asserted, and the inventory was undertaken as follows.*

Items [12]	rd	sh	rs	rd	sh	rs
Ironware						
1 big kettle	24					
1 d:o smaller	16					
1 steel pot	4					
1 frying pan	8					
1 poker	4					
1 hand ax	8					
1 chopping ax	6					
1 d:o worse	5					
1 spade	8					
2 augers	1	6				
1 hide switch [for softening hides]	0	6				
1 planting hook	2					
1 hammer and tongs	2					
1 hand saw	0	6				
1 d:o better	1					

---

[10] March 25 according to the Death and Funeral Register.

[11] At this time, widows were the only women with property rights.

[12] The value of the items are given in rd = riksdaler, sh = shilling and rs = rundstycken. 1 riksdaler = 48 shilling, 1 shilling = 12 rundstycken.

1 wood planer	2				
1 razor... (?)	3				
1 carving knife ... (?)	0	6			
3 buckles	1		2	1	0
Vats, basins and buckets					
1 vat	8				
1 bucket no. 1	8				
1 d:o no. 2	8				
1 d:o no. 3	2				
1 d:o no. 4	1				
1 bucket no. 5	1				
1 d:o no. 6	3				
1 bear barrel	8				
1 cabbage barrel	10				
1 herring trough	2				
1 water trough	4				
1 d:o worse	3				
1 water tub	1				
2 d:o worse	1				
2 soaking tubs	2				
2 d:o	2				
3 winnowing troughs	2				
3 wooden plates	2				
1 wooden tankard	1				
1 square "sätting" [= ½ bushel]	2				
1 square bushel	2				
1 loom	8				
1 spinning wheel	6				
1 reeling frame	0	6			
2 manure forks	1				
1 sled	4				
1 grindstone	1				

1 hand mill		8		2	4	6
Chests						
1 big chest		16				
1 d:o worse		4				
1 rope basket			6			
1 flax scutcher		1			21	6
Men's clothes						
1 grey coat	1					
1 d:o worse		12				
1 grey vest		16				
1 short sweater		8				
1 bodice		4				
1 pair of leather pants		8				
3 pairs of old ones		1				
2 better shirts		16				
2 d:o		16				
1 d:o worse		2				
1 par grey socks		8				
1 black hat		6				
1 d:o worse			6			
1 old hymnbook		3		3	2	6
The widow's clothes						
were examined and evaluated to	1			1		
Animals						
1 sheep without lamb		16				
2 pigs		8			24	
Some straw and hay		40			40	
Total				9	44	6

Estate debts		
To the usher Anders Pärsson of Mar-kustorp for purchase at auction	*16*	
To Johan Larsson of Nedre Holmen for one bushel of malt	*36*	
To Erik Månsson of Nedre Holmen for one day of plowing	*24*	
D:o to the same man for feeding one sheep	*20*	
D:o to Jon Pärsson of Granhögen	*20*	
1/8 poverty percent [a form of tax]		*6*
Fee to district judge Warderi	*8*	
My fee for two copies of this inven-tory	*16*	
Total	*2 42*	*6*

If required, I can confirm by oath that nothing is intentionally concealed but everything so declared as it was at the hour of death.

Kirsti Segolsdotter
Johan Jonsson

We confirm that everything is registered as it is

Anders Månsson, Nedre Holmen
Lars Andersson, district taxation registrar

The one-eighth percent for relief of the poor was paid with 6 rundstycken in cash by Anders Månsson.

Comments

Several miscalculations appear in the estate inventory:

- For "Vats, basins and buckets" the sum should be 2.5.6, not 2.4.6.
- For "Men's clothes" the sum should be 3.4.6, not 3.2.6.
- For "Estate debts" the sum should be 2.44.6, not 2.42.6.

Estate inventory after Kerstin Segolsdotter (1752-1804) [403]

(Read more about this inventory on page 43)

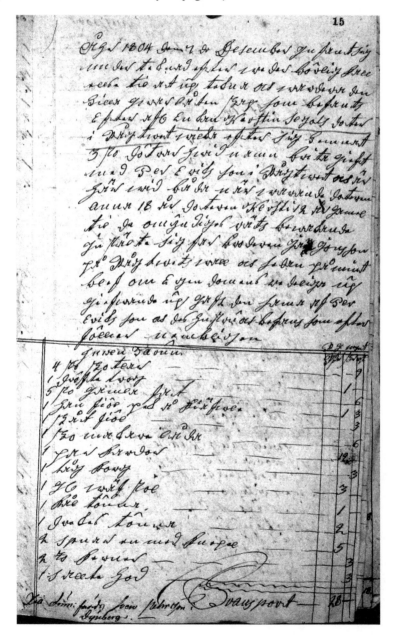

<u>English translation</u>

On December 7, 1804, the undersigned [executor] appeared, after due request, to register and evaluate the little estate that remained after the deceased widow Kerstin Segolsdotter in Rågtvet, who has left behind three daughters by the names of Britta, married to Per Eriksson of Rågtvet who are both here present, the daughter Anna, 18 years, and the daughter Kirsti, 12 years old. To guard the rights of the under age [daughters], their uncle Jan Jonsson from Rågtvets Vall appeared, and since instructions had been given regarding the honest declaration of the estate, the above mentioned Per Eriksson and his wife declared the estate which was found as follows.

	rd	sh	rs
... (?)	-		
4 "skotlar" (?)			9
1 winnowing trough		1	
5 old plates			6
1 bread shovel and rolling pin		1	3
1 bread shovel with long handle			3
1 shoemaker's toolbox			6
1 pair of carding combs		12	
1 rope basket			3
1 old loom		3	
1 cabbage barrel		1	
1 ...barrel (?)		2	
2 ... with fastener (?)		5	
2 rolling pins			3
1 salting trough			3
1 milk tub			3
1 reeling frame		1	
1 grain sieve		1	
1 hand mill		12	
1 tub		2	

1 bottle	*1*	
1 spade	*2*	
1 pot with handle	*12*	
1 old ... pan (?)		*3*
1 "hakehod" (?)	*1*	
1 old ax	*2*	
1 pair of sheep shears		*3*
1 drill		*3*
1 dram glass without foot		*8*
2 wooden plates		*3*
1 chest	*16*	*?*
1 casket	*4*	*?*
2 old weaver's reeds	*2*	*?*
1 carving knife		*?*
2 old spinning wheels	*2*	*?*
1 tobacco pouch and 2 wallets	*3*	*?*
1 folding knife	*1*	*?*
1 clothes-brush and tinder box		*?*
1 old hymnbook		*?*
1 old "sädesbolla" (?)		*?*
1 old saw without bow		*?*
Women's clothes		
1 old ... hat (?)	*1*	*?*
1 black silk cloth	*16*	*?*
2 white cotton cloths	*28*	*?*
3 linen cloths	*8*	*?*
1 calico apron	*16*	*?*
1 white d:o	*8*	*?*
1 common d:o	*6*	*?*
6 linen cloths	*40*	*?*
1 top	*3*	*?*
1 linen tick	*24*	*?*

2 old bedcovers	3		
1 blue homespun sweater	32		
2 old d:o	3		
1 skein of linen yarn	6		
1 old blue grogram skirt	24		
1 blue ordinary d:o	4		
2 old d:o	6		
Grains			
2 half bushels of oats	32		
1 half bushel of peas	20		
1 bag	1		
2 old bodices	4		
1 rotten shed with a small chamber	24		
Demands			
From Anders Månsson in Holmen for a loan dated October 30, 1800	4	8	
Overdue interest rate	1	1	4
Total	12	29	1

Debts		
To Jon Mauritsson of Rågtvet for making and transporting the coffin	1	16
1/2 hundred nails for d:o		6
For one bushel of rye for the funeral	2	
2 "marker" butter for d:o[13]		16
4 d:o cheese		18
Meat for d:o		16
Fee for the estate inventory		28
D:o to the district judge		16

---

[13] One mark (plural: marker) was an old weight measure = 340 grams.

Share to the poor			9
For the District Court's signature		16	
Total	5	36	9

If required, we can confirm by oath that nothing is intentionally concealed.

Per Eriksson
Brita Olofsdotter

This is how everything was registered and valued testify

Anders Persson, Usher
Lars Jonsson, Juryman of Rågtvet
Jan Jonsson, from Rågtvets Vall on behalf of the under aged

Comment

One page of the inventory is folded in such a way that one can not read the rightmost column where the value in rundstycken is registered (replaced with question marks above). Thus, it is not possible to completely verify if the different posts are correctly summarized or not. However, it seems probable the total sum of the assets should be 13.29.1, not 12.29.1.

Estate inventory after Jonas Eriksson (1812-1864) [404]

(Read more about this inventory on page 108)

English translation

On February 7, 1865, after due request, the undersigned [executors] *performed legal estate inventory after the sawmill worker Jonas Eriksson at Stavre Mosse by Trollhättan, who gave in to death last October 18, and left behind his widow Kajsa Andersson and, in his previous marriage together with his also previously deceased wife Karolina Svensdotter conceived children, the sons Edvard and Johan Fredrik, of age and living in Stockholm, the son Carl, born on July 24, 1847, and the daughter Johanna Sofia, born on May 15, 1850, both under age, who's rights were guarded by their legally assigned custodian, the tailor Olaus Svensson from Trollhättan, who also guarded the rights and benefits of the older sons living in Stockholm. According to chapter 9 of the Inheritance Law, the widow was by oath instructed to declare the assets and debts of the estate as they were at the death hour of her husband, which happened in the following order.*

14	*rdr*	*öre*	*rdr*	*öre*
Assets				
One dwelling house at Stavre Mosse			*200*	
Tin objects				
1 bottle, 1 measuring cup		*50*		
1 coffee pot, 2 coffee hats		*50*	*1*	
Iron wear				
2 pots	*2*			
1 frying pan, 1 pair of fire tongs, 1 fire ring	*1*			
2 axes		*75*		
1 padlock, 1 hammer, 1 pair of tongs, 1 auger		*25*	*4*	

---

[14] The monetary units shilling and rundstycken have now been replaced by öre. 1 riksdaler = 100 öre.

Furniture				
1 wall clock	*3*			
1 table	*1*	*50*		
1 cupboard	*3*			
1 chest of drawers		*75*		
1 sofa	*2*			
1 bed with bedclothes	*2*		*12*	*25*
Clothes of the deceased				
1 old coat	*3*			
1 pair of pants, 1 pair of suspenders	*2*			
1 vest		*75*		
2 hats		*50*		
1 scarf, 1 shirtfront		*25*		
Various old clothes		*75*	*7*	*25*
Miscellaneous				
4 half curtains	*1*			
8 empty bottles		*35*		
½ dozen plates of china		*75*		
1 carafe, 1 cream pitcher, 2 drinking, 2 dram glasses	*1*	*25*		
1 butter plate, 1 sugar urn		*25*		
Various baking utensils		*75*		
2 carving knives		*25*		
1 breadboard with knife		*10*		
1 sledge	*1*	*25*		
1 water bucket with yoke, 1 basin		*75*		
4 chairs	*1*			
9 rose cans with whale-oil		*50*		
5 coffee cups, 1 tray	*1*			
1 flat iron		*50*		
1 water basin, 1 salt tub	*1*	*25*		

1 drop-leaf table, 1 smaller d:o	2	50		
1 sewing box, 2 paintings		25		
1 coffee grinder, 1 pair of carding combs		50		
4 stone plates, 1 cup, 1 saltcellar, 1 plate	1			
1 fork hammer, 1 brick trowel, 1 mason's level		25		
1 lantern, 1 coffee roaster, 1 pot, 1 chopping trough	1	50		
1 bed rack, 1 footstool, 1 breadbasket, 1 pot	1			
Hinges for one window		15		
1 pair of boots, 2 pair of gloves, 1 trunk	3	25		
2 clothes-brushes, 1 bottle, 1 tin measuring cup		25		
1 drinking water barrel		75		
1 swine animal	5	25		
Half of one rowing-boat	3		30	60
Total in riksdaler national currency			255	10

Debts				
To Mr. John Svensson Trollhättan	90	55		
To Mr. A. J. Petterson ibidem	36	45		
To Mr. O. A. Lindblom	11	87		
To A. Högvall rest of promissory note dated July 7, 1858	3	62		
To Madam Hällgren	1	25		
To the sawmill worker Olaus Stollt		54		
To the widow Maria Fernström	1			
Fee for the estate inventory	3		148	28
Estate balance			106	82
Total in riksdaler national currency			255	10

I testify under obligation by oath that this estate has been correctly and honestly declared such as it was at the death hour of my husband and that not the smallest part of it has been intentionally concealed or left out.

Kajsa Andersson
with hand on pen

During this procedure I have been present

as above

Olaus Svensson
with hand on pen

As inventory and evaluation executers sign

A. I. Pettersson
L. Arfvedsson

Estate inventory after Johannes Svensson (1839-1903) [405]

(Read more about this inventory on page 123)

English translation

On September 7, 1903, estate inventory was performed after the home owner Johannes Svensson in Trollhättan, who passed away there on June 2 of the same year, leaving as part owners of the estate the widow Maria Kristina Svensson and the major children Frithiof Julius, Ivar Ferdinand, Gustaf Henning, Amalia Sofia, Johan Albin, Karl Hilding, Sven Fingal, and Johannes Emanuel, and the minor daughters Jenny Emilia, Elin Viktoria, and Hilma Fredrika, whose rights were guarded by their custodian, the worker Sven August Malmqvist of Trollhättan.

The estate, which was declared by the widow under obligation of oath, was registered and valued in the following order:

[15]	kr	öre	kr	öre
Assets				
One residential building on unfree ground in the block Diana No. 4	*400*			
One d:o on d:o	*200*			
One common shed on d:o	*50*		*650*	
Household equipment				
Various copper vessels	*3*			
Various iron vessels	*6*	*50*		
Various tin vessels	*1*			
Various glass and porcelain	*3*			
Various lamps	*2*			
Various knives, forks and spoons	*1*			
Various baking utensils	*2*	*50*		
Various barrels	*1*		*20*	
Furniture				

---

[15] The monetary unit riksdaler has now been replaced by crowns. 1 crown = 100 öre.

2 chests of drawers, 1 dresser	9	50		
5 old wooden settles, 1 mirror	6	60		
1 table, 6 chairs	5			
1 American wall clock	5			
1 bed with bedclothes	10		33	50
Miscellaneous				
Various bedclothes	10			
Various sheets and bed covers	5			
Various towels	3			
Various curtains and carpets	3			
Various shoemaker's tools	10			
Various not itemized	5			
One old sewing machine	10		46	
The clothing was valued to			31	
Crowns			780	50

Subtracted from this				
Funeral costs	50			
Doctor and medicine	10			
Municipality tax	7	74	67	74
Balance in crown			712	76

According to declaration registered and valued, verify
Pehr Ersson   K. A. Selander
Inventory executers

I testify under obligation by oath that this estate was correctly declared and nothing intentionally concealed or left out.
                    Maria Kristina Svensdotter

We declare ourselves satisfied with all parts of the preceding estate inventory
F. J. Fridén, Ivar F. Landgren, Amalia Sofia Svensson, Gustaf Henning Landgren, Johan Albin Svensson, Karl Hilding Landgren, Sven Fingal Svensson, Johannes Svensson, August Malmqvist

Letters regarding the disappearance of Olof Westerlind [406]

English translation

Exhibi Gothenburg Cathedral Chapter, September 15, 1796 [16]

Reverend Doctor and Bishop, Commander of the Royal Order of the Polar Star, one of the Eighteen Members of the Swedish Academy, and Maxime Venerandum Consistorium [= Highly Venerable Cathedral Chapter].

The soldier Olof Westerlind, about whom, in a highly celebrated writing dated the 9th of this month, information is asked for, has, since, in 1783, he was dismissed from the service of the King and Crown, rapidly left town, without requiring a transition certificate from the parish office. They say that he has found his way to Uddevalla, where rumors claim that he has married, since a formal notification of missing had been made after his escaped wife, who, in the certificate with which Westerlind arrived here in 1782, is called Karin Carlsdotter. Where he is now residing nobody knows, if not in his birth place which is Tunhem Parish in Västergötland.

With deep reverence insists the humble servant of Reverend Doctor and Bishop, Commander of the Royal Order of the Polar Star, one of the Eighteen Members of the Swedish Academy, and Maxime Venerandum Consistorium

Tanum, August 29, 1796

Assistant Vicar Brunius

Comment

There are two mistakes in Assistant Vicar Brunius' letter:

- Olof Westerlind was not dismissed from Bohuslän Light Dragoon Regiment in 1783 but at the General Muster of June 26, 1788.

- Olof Westerlind did not marry in Uddevalla but in Västra Tunhem on August 4, 1787.

---

[16] This note is added by the Cathedral Chapter and corresponds to the present day official recording and archiving of incoming mail.

Högwördigste och Vidtberömde Herr Doctor och Biskop,
Commendeur af Kongelige Nordstjerne Orden,
En af de Aderton i Swenska Academien,
                    samt
Maxime Venerandum Consistorium.

Til ödmjukaste svar å höggunstiga skrifelsen af d. 15 den-
nes, som jag i dag undfick, länder at afskedade Dragonen Olof Wästerlind icke är gift här i församlingen, men at han d. 28

Augusti 1787 presenterade Prästbevis utfärdadt af Aflidne
Kyrkoherden Helltenius i Junkhen, at innehåll af Wästerlind och hans hustru Elin Swensdotter ägde någorlunda för-
svarlig Christendoms Kundskap och nyttjat nådamedlen;
hwilket Prästbevis de d. 20 Maji 1789 fingo påskrifvit af mig
til Junkhen.
    Detta är all den uplysning, som jag om ofvannämnde
Dragons giftermål och vistande kan hafva den äran at
afgifva.
    Med djupaste vördnad har äran af framlefva.

Högvördigste och Vidtberömde Herr Doctors,
        Biskopens och Commendeurens
                    samt
Maxime Venerandi Consistorii.

Uddevalla d. 20 Sept.   allerödmjukaste tjänare
        1796.   Matthias Schröder.

158

English translation

Exhibi Gothenburg Cathedral Chapter, October 12, 1796

Reverend and Widely Renowned Doctor and Bishop, Commander of the Royal Order of the Polar Star, one of the Eighteen Members of the Swedish Academy, and Maxime Venerandum Consistorium.

As a most humble answer to the highly celebrated writing of the 15th of this month, which I received today, comes out that the dismissed dragoon Olof Wästerlind was certainly not married in this parish but that he, on August 28, 1787, presented a transition certificate issued by the deceased vicar Helstenius of Tunhem, containing the information that O Wästerlind and his wife Elin Svensdotter possessed reasonably satisfactory scripture knowledge and had attended Holy Communion, which transition certificate I, on May 20, 1789, signed for them for their transition to Tunhem.

This is all the information about the wedding and the residence of the above mentioned dragoon I have the honor of conveying.

With deepest reverence having the honor of presenting to Reverend and Widely Renowned Doctor, Bishop, and Commander of the Royal Order of the Polar Star, and Maxime Venerandum Consistorium.

Uddevalla, September 20, 1796

Most humble servant
Mattias Schröder

Where to find sources for genealogical studies

This book is based on thorough genealogical studies. Most of the sources for these studies are available on the Internet. To inspire and assist those of my readers, who would like to perform similar studies of their own families, I here supply some short comments about the main sources that I have used. I am well aware that the information I can offer is incomplete, since

– my studies only involve genealogical sources in Sweden,

– in the ever-growing Internet community, there may well be sources that I am not aware of, and

– the sources that I am referring to will most certainly continue developing after I have published this book.

ArkivDigital, https://www.arkivdigital.se/
This was my main source of information. It is the largest provider of Swedish historical records online, such as Church Records, Court Records, Military Records, Tax Registers, and Estate Inventories. All documents are photographed with modern technique and in color. The images as such are sharp and clear, but interpreting handwriting from the 18th century and further back requires practice. ArkivDigital is growing continuously as more images are being added. A one year subscription costs about US$ 175. Shorter periods for a lower price are also available.

The National Archives, https://sok.riksarkivet.se/
The National Archives, or "Riksarkivet" in Swedish, is a state institution which consists of a number of archives located in different parts of Sweden. Together, they store an innumerable amount of historical documents, all listed in extensive registers on the home page of the National Archives. There you will also find a minor part of the documents photographed in black and white. More documents can be accessed by visiting the libraries of the local archives where they are stored. I have mainly read documents from the National Archives via Internet, but I was

several times unable to find a certain entry in their registers by means of the search engine on their home page. To my surprise, using Google sometimes seemed to be more effective. ArkivDigital has photographed a minor part of the documents from the National Archives and the number is continually growing. At present, a six months' subscription with the National Archives costs about US$ 60, but will probably soon be rendered free of charge.

Ancestry, https://www.ancestry.com/
I have little experience of this source of information, since I have only used it to trace two family members (not mentioned in this book) who emigrated to America. It is focused on the genealogy of Americans, and can be of essential help to find a connection to your roots in Europe. However, once you have found an ancestor in Sweden, I would trace the rest of this family branch by means of the more complete ArkivDigital. The price of a six months' full membership with Ancestry is US$ 199.

Rötter, https://www.genealogi.se/
Rötter (= Roots) is the home page of Sveriges släktforskarförbund (= the Genealogical Research Association of Sweden). The home page offers valuable information on how to trace your ancestors in Sweden.

Släktdata, http://www.slaktdata.org/index.php/regsearch
Släktdata is an association of volunteers, who transcribe the hand-written Church Records to make them searchable over the Internet. Some geographical areas are well-covered, others not at all. With some luck, Släktdata can be a fast way of finding relatives by name and home parish, but the transcripts are not complete and sometimes contain errors. The use is free of charge.

Central Soldier Register, http://www.soldatreg.se/sok-soldat/
The Central Soldier Register, "Centrala soldatregistret", contains name, company, homestead, etc. of 500 000 soldiers who served in different military units under the so-called allotment system

between 1682 and 1901. Just like Släktdata, the Central Soldier Register can be a way of finding an entry to one's family, simply entering a name and a home parish. Free of charge.

Sveriges befolkning (= Sweden's population) is a series of data bases containing transcripts of the results of national censuses from 1880 through 1990. Some of them are available on Internet via ArkivDigital's home page, but most of them can only be bought on CD, for example at http://webbutik.riksarkivet.se/se/. Similarly, **Sveriges dödbok** (= Sweden's death register) is a transcript of the death registers from 1901 through 2013, available on CD. These data bases cover the whole population of the country and are easily searchable, but may – since they are transcribed – contain single errors. The price of the CD:s varies between US$ 50 and 75 a piece.

Information about the **present day inhabitants of Sweden** is available over the Internet by means of search engines like www.eniro.se, www.birthday.se and www.upplysning.se. Children under 18 and people who have been given so-called protected identities due to threats etc. are not listed. All these search engines can be used free of charge.

The Stockholm University Map Room,
http://kartavdelningen.sub.su.se/kartrummet/default.htm
The Map Room, or "Kartrummet", of Stockholm University holds a series of historical, economic maps from different judicial districts in Sweden. The maps were drawn in the late 19th century and are available for free over the Internet.

The Land Survey Board Archives,
https://etjanster.lantmateriet.se/historiskakartor/s/advancedsearch.html
The Land Survey Board Archives, or "Lantmäteristyrelsens arkiv", contains historical maps. What has been most useful in my research are the detailed maps from the redistributions of land, which are set up homestead by homestead, parish by parish. With each map comes the minutes from the redistribution meet-

ing, where the names of the land owners are listed. The documents are available for free over the Internet.

Eniro, https://kartor.eniro.se/

Aside from being a search engine for addresses and phone numbers in present day Sweden, Eniro also offers detailed maps where even names of single farms can be found. Since geographical names tend to live for centuries, there is a good chance that the Eniro maps can help you find farms dating back to the 18th and 19th century. The use of Eniro is free.

Notes

BBR = Birth and Baptism Register ("Födelse och dopbok")
BMR = Banns and Marriage Register ("Lysnings och vigsel-bok")
CHR = Catechetical Hearing Register ("Husförhörslängd")
CR = Congregation Register ("Församlingsbok")
DFR = Death and Funeral Register ("Död och begravningsbok")
PR = Person Register ("Personregister")
RR = Relocation Register ("In- och utflyttningslängd")
TR = Tax Register ("Mantalslängd")

---

[1] https://kartor.eniro.se/

[2] Hedlund, Oscar: *Kyrkolivet i Karlstads stift under 1800-talets förra hälft*, Lund University, 1949.

[3] National Economic Maps, Elfsborg Province, Sundal Judicial District – eastern part, 1895. Map room, Stockholm University.

[4] Sundal Judicial District Estate Inventories 1736-39 (FIIa:1), p. 53 f.

[5] Gestad CHR 1761-67 (AI:1), p. 7.

[6] Bolstad BBR 1763-1833 (C:1), p. 3, serial no. 12. Born July 4, baptized July 5, 1763. Witnesses: Engebret Ersson of Simonstorp and Kerstin Andersdotter of Rågtvet.

[7] Bolstad DFR 1763-1811 (F:1), p. 3, serial no. 1. Dead January 9, 1763. Cause of death: stomach disease.

[8] Bolstad DFR 1763-1811 (F:1), p. 39, serial no. 30. Dead April 24, 1772. Cause of death: tuberculosis.

[9] Bolstad DFR 1763-1811 (F:1), p. 59, serial no. 30. Dead August 14, 1774. Cause of death: pneumonia.

[10] Sundal Judicial District Estate Inventories 1775-76 (FIIa:18), p. 37-45.

[11] Gestad CHR 1774-80 (AI:3), p. 8.

[12] Land Survey Board Archive, Gestad parish, Simonstorp, Great Redistribution of infields, 1785.

[13] Gestad CHR 1768-74 (AI:2), p. 9. The son Anders is not in the BBR.

[14] Gestad BBR 1763-1833 (C:1), p. 41, serial no. 21. Born September 4, baptized September 8, 1775. Witnesses: Engebret Nilsson (should be Ersson)

of Simonstorp and Siri Andersdotter of Slommehagen. The name of the mother is noted to be Britta Hansdotter instead of Botilla Andersdotter, but the name of the child, the name of the father and the dwelling place are all correct. Since similar mistakes appear several times, it seems likely that the pastor was hard of hearing.

[15] Gestad CHR 1774-80 (AI:3), p. 8.

[16] Bolstad DFR 1763-1811 (F:1), p. 157, serial no. 7. Dead March 9, 1788. Cause of death: pneumonia.

[17] Bolstad DFR 1763-1811 (F:1), p. 173, serial no. 51. Dead April 2, 1790. Cause of death: mortal disease.

[18] Gestad CHR 1774-80 (AI:3), p. 73.

[19] Daniel Larsson: *Den dolda transitionen - Om ett demografiskt brytnings-skede i det tidiga 1700-talets Sverige*, Historical Institution, Gothenburg University, Gothenburg 2006.

[20] Gestad BBR 1763-1833 (C:1), p. 53, serial no. 7. Born February 28, baptized March 1, 1778. Witnesses: Tolle Hansson of Slommehagen and Brita Andersdotter of Simonstorp. Here, too, the name of the mother has been misheard and is noted to be Svensdotter instead of Halvardsdotter, but everything else is correct: the name of the child, the name of the father, the dwelling place and even the witnesses.

[21] Gestad CHR 1774-80 (AI:3), p. 18.

[22] Gestad BBR 1763-1833 (C:1), p. 69, serial no. 18. Born April 4, baptized April 8, 1780. Witnesses: Eric Segolsson of Balltorp and Botilla Andersdotter of Simonstorp.

[23] General Muster roll 1789, picture 92-94. Västgöta-Dal Regiment, Sundal Company, Forth Corporalship.

[24] Gestad CHR 1781-86 (AI:4), p. 13, and Gestad CHR 1787-95 (AI:5), p. 31.

[25] Gestad BBR 1763-1833 (C:1), p. 113, serial no. 31. Born July 26, baptized July 27, 1788. Witnesses: Erik Segolsson of Balltorp and Ingri Segolsdotter of Simonstorp.

[26] Bolstad DFR 1763-1811 (F:1), p. 158, serial no. 23. Dead September 28, 1788. Cause of death: unknown disease. The child's name is noted to be Karin, not Kerstin, but everything else is correct, and there was no other child by the last name of Olsdotter at Simonstorp Stom in 1788.

[27] Gestad CHR 1787-95 (AI:5), p. 14.

[28] Bolstad DFR 1763-1811 (F:1), p. 172, serial no. 7. Dead January 10, 1790. Cause of death: stomach disease. The last name i noted to be Olofsdotter, not Halvardsdotter, but the pastor has probably misheard the name, since only one Ingbor died at Brettorp Stom that year.

[29] Gestad BBR 1763-1833 (C:1), p. 147, serial no. 18. Eric, Born April 25, baptized April 27, 1794 at Simonstorp. Witnesses: Johan Segolsson and the wife Karin Larsdotter of Simonstorp.
Gestad BBR 1763-1833 (C:1), p. 173, serial no. 30. Caisa, Born September 25, baptized September 26, 1798 at Stenviken. Witnesses: Sven Andersson and Caisa Venerberg of Lillebyn (Bolstad), Johan Segolsson of Bäckehagen and the wife Caisa Jacobsdotter of Höketorp.

[30] Gestad CHR 1787-95 (AI:5), p. 25.

[31] Gestad CHR 1796-1803 (AI:6), p. 49.

[32] Bolstad DFR 1763-1811 (F:1), p. 232, serial no. 26 and 28. Dead July 11 and July 17, 1799, respectively. Cause of death for both: tuberculosis.

[33] Gestad CHR 1796-1803 (AI:6), p. 45.

[34] Gestad CHR 1804-08 (AI:7), p. 31.

[35] Gestad CHR 1804-08 (AI:7), p. 50.

[36] Gestad CHR 1804-08 (AI:7), p. 187.

[37] Gestad CHR 1804-08 (AI:7), p. 94.

[38] Gestad CHR 1809-13 (AI:8), p. 69.

[39] Gestad CHR 1809-13 (AI:8), p. 6.

[40] *Historiskt-geografiskt och statistiskt lexikon öfver Sverige*, Volume 5 (1859-1870), p. 389, headword: Qvantensburg.
http://runeberg.org/hgsl/5/0391.html

[41] National Economic Maps, Elfsborg Province, Sundal Judicial District – eastern part, 1895. Map room, Stockholm University.

[42] TR 1642-1820 Älvsborg Province, year 1744, p. 252.

[43] Bolstad CHR 1768-74 (AI:1), p. 109.

[44] TR 1642-1820 Älvsborg Province, year 1750, p. 261.

[45] TR 1642-1820 Älvsborg Province, year 1758, p. 364.

[46] TR 1642-1820 Älvsborg Province, year 1760, p. 350.

[47] TR 1642-1820 Älvsborg Province, year 1761, p. 349.

[48] TR 1642-1820 Älvsborg Province, year 1762, p. 307.

[49] TR 1642-1820 Älvsborg Province, year 1764, p. 359.

[50] TR 1642-1820 Älvsborg Province, year 1765:1, p. 337.

[51] TR 1642-1820 Älvsborg Province, year 1766, p. 355.

[52] TR 1642-1820 Älvsborg Province, year 1767, p. 361.

[53] TR 1642-1820 Älvsborg Province, year 1768, p. 346.

[54] TR 1642-1820 Älvsborg Province, year 1769, p. 353.

[55] Bolstad CHR 1768-74 (AI:1), p. 108.

[56] TR 1642-1820 Älvsborg Province, year 1770, p. 268.

[57] TR 1642-1820 Älvsborg Province, year 1771, p. 313.

[58] TR 1642-1820 Älvsborg Province, year 1772, p. 349.

[59] Bolstad DFR 1763-1811 (F:1).

[60] Grimberg, Carl: Svenska folkets underbara öden - VI. Frihetstidens höjd-punkt och slut 1739-1772 (1913-1939), p. 606 f.

[61] TR 1642-1820 Älvsborg Province, year 1774, p. 397.

[62] TR 1642-1820 Älvsborg Province, year 1775:1, p. 438.

[63] TR 1642-1820 Älvsborg Province, year 1776:1, p. 414.

[64] TR 1642-1820 Älvsborg Province, year 1777, p. 402.

[65] Land Survey Board Archive, Gestad parish, Björnerud, Great Redistribution of fields, 1773.

[66] Gestad CHR 1761-67 (AI:1), p. 45.

[67] Gestad CHR 1768-74 (AI:2), p. 57.

[68] Bolstad DFR 1763-1811 (F:1), p. 27, serial no. 7. Dead April 21, 1770. Cause of death: rapid disease.

[69] Sundals Judicial Districts Estate Inventories 1769-71 (FIIa:14), p. 443.

[70] Bolstad BMR 1763-1840 (E:1), p. 23, year 1771, serial no. 1. The name of the bride has been misheard as Anna Olofsdotter.

[71] TR 1642-1820 Älvsborg Province, year 1772, p. 365.

[72] Gestad BBR 1763-1833 (C:1), p. 29, serial no. 4. Born February 28, baptized February 30 (sic!), 1772. Witnesses: Bryngel Andersson and Lisbet Michelsdotter of Björnerud.

[73] Bolstad DFR 1763-1811 (F:1), p. 39, serial no. 21 and 22 respectively. Dead April 25 1772. Cause of death: childbirth and unknown child disease respectively.

[74] Land Survey Board Archive, Gestad parish, Björnerud, Great Redistribution of fields, 1773.

[75] TR 1642-1820 Älvsborg Province, year 1774, p. 414.

[76] Gestad CHR 1768-74 (AI:2), p. 57.

[77] Gestad CHR 1774-80 (AI:3), p. 49.

[78] Gestad BBR 1763-1833 (C:1), p. 43, serial no. 32. Born November 16, baptized November 19, 1775. Witnesses: Jon Jonsson and Kerstin Larsdotter of Björnerud.

[79] Gestad CHR 1768-74 (AI:2), p. 74.

[80] TR 1642-1820 Älvsborg Province, year 1776:1, p. 433

[81] Gestad CHR 1781-86 (AI:4), p. 74.

[82] Land Survey Board Archive, Gestad parish, Björnerud, Investigation regarding the ownership of certain grounds, 1784.

[83] Gestad CHR 1774-80 (AI:3), p. 21.

[84] Bolstad CHR 1781-86 (AI:2), p. 153. Bolstads CHR 1775-80 missing!

[85] TR 1642-1820 Älvsborg Province, year 1779, p. 357.

[86] Bolstad CHR 1781-86 (AI:2), p. 150.

[87] Bolstad BBR 1763-1833 (C:1), p. 81, serial no. 23. Born August 13, baptized August 14, 1781. Witnesses: Per Andersson and Kari Hansdotter, Holmen.

[88] Bolstad BBR 1763-1833 (C:1), p. 82, serial no. 31. Born and baptized October 26,1781. Witnesses: Anders Jonsson of Holmen and Annika Månsdotter of Tillhagen.

[89] Bolstad DFR 1763-1811 (F:1), p. 114, serial no. 44. Dead August 25, 1782. Cause of death: throat disease.

[90] Bolstad DFR 1763-1811 (F:1), p. 122, serial no. 50. Dead September 15, 1782. Cause of death: smallpox.

[91] Bolstad BBR 1763-1833 (C:1), p. 94, serial no. 16. Born August 25, baptized August 27, 1783. Witnesses: Erik Larson and Kerstin Bengtsdotter of Holmen.

[92] Bolstad CHR 1781-86 (AI:2), p. 181.

[93] Bolstad CHR 1787-96 (AI:3), p. 228.

[94] Grinstad CHR 1787-95 (AI:8), p. 221.

[95] Gestad CHR 1787-95 (AI:5), p. 146.

[96] Bolstad DFR 1763-1811 (F:1), p. 148, serial no. 10. Dead May 1, 1788. Cause of death: pneumonia.

[97] Land Survey Board Archive, Bolstad parish, Höga, Great Redistribution of fields, 1787.

[98] Bolstad CHR 1787-96 (AI:3), p. 286.

[99] Bolstad BBR 1763-1833 (C:1), p. 127, serial no. 17. Born August 1, baptized August 2, 1789. Witnesses: Lars Segolsson and Katarina Månsdotter of Höga.

[100] Bolstad DFR 1763-1811 (F:1) p. 223, serial no. 6. Dead March 25, 1798. Cause of death: dysentery.

[101] Bolstad CHR 1796-1803 (AI:4), p. 150.

[102] Bolstad DFR 1763-1811 (F:1), p. 231, serial no. 6. Dead February 24, 1799. Cause of death: rapid disease.

[103] Bolstad CHR 1796-1803 (AI:4), p. 159.

[104] Grinstad CHR 1795-1803 (AI:9), p. 154.

[105] Bolstad BMR 1763-1840 (E:1), p. 163, year 1803, serial no. 7.

[106] Gestad CHR 1804-08 (AI:7), p. 2.

[107] Bolstad CHR 1804-08 (AI:5), p. 156.

[108] Bolstad CHR 1796-1803 (AI:4), p. 109 and Bolstad CHR 1804-08 (AI:5), p. 119.

[109] Gestad CHR 1804-08 (AI:7), p. 2.

[110] Bolstad CHR 1804-08 (AI:5), p. 126 and Bolstad CHR 1809-13 (AI:6), p. 85.

[111] Gestad CHR 1809-13 (AI:8), p. 2.

[112] The place of birth can be found in Gestad CHR 1842-46 (AI:14), p. 9.

[113] Land Survey Board Archive, Gestad parish, Rågtvet, Great Redistribution, 1764.

[114] TR 1642-1820 Älvsborg Province, year 1805, p. 922.

[115] TR 1642-1820 Älvsborg Province, year 1806, p. 1022-1025.

[116] Hambré, Mikael: *Herr Christer G. Zelows plan af ladugården i Rågtvet.* The Royal Swedish Academy of Agriculture and Forestry, 1816, p. 204 ff.

[117] Land Survey Board Archive, Gestad parish, Rågtvet, Redistribution of land, 1827.

[118] Gestad CHR 1809-13 (AI:8), p. 139.

[119] Gestad BBR 1763-1833 (C:1), p. 259, serial no. 18. Born May 4, baptized May 6, 1812. Witnesses: Olof Jonsson and Maja Nilsdotter of Parken.

[120] Gestad CHR 1809-13 (AI:8), p. 6.

[121] Gestad CHR 1814-18 (AI:9), p. 6.

[122] Gestad BBR 1763-1833 (C:1), p. 275, serial no. 29. Born May 2, baptized May 4, 1815. Witnesses: the soldier Jan Lustig and Cajsa Persdotter of Simonstorp Stom. The dwelling place of the mother is erroneously noted to be Simonstorp.

[123] Bolstad DFR 1812-45 (F:2), p. 24, serial no. 4. Dead February 26, March buried 3, 1816. Cause of death not stated.

[124] Bolstad BMR 1763-1840 (E:1), p. 233, year 1816.

[125] Gestad CHR 1814-18 (AI:9), p. 19.

[126] Photo: Bertil Martinsson, Tvings Långasjö Local History Society.

[127] Gestad CHR 1824-29 (AI:11), p. 91.

[128] Gestad CHR 1829-35 (AI:12), p. 13.

[129] Land Survey Board Archive, Gestad parish, Balltorp, Legal Redistribution of infields, 1831.

[130] Land Survey Board Archive, Gestad parish, Simonstorp, Legal Redistribution of infields, 1834.

[131] Gestad CHR 1814-18 (AI:9), p. 19.

[132] Gestad BBR 1763-1833 (C:1), p. 287, serial no. 25. Born June 13, baptized June 16, 1817. Witnesses: Hans Ersson and Lisbeth Bryngelsdotter, Balltorp.

[133] Bolstad DFR 1812-45 (F:2), p. 27, serial no. 21. The death date is noted to be June 29, 1817. Most probably it should be July 29, 1817, since the funeral service was held on August 3, and the age of the boy is said to be two months. Cause of death: stomach disease.

[134] Gestad BBR 1763-1833 (C:1), p. 292, serial no. 20. Born June 30, baptized July 3, 1818. Witnesses: Olof Andersson and Stina Svensdotter, Bredtorp.

[135] Gestad BBR 1763-1833 (C:1), p. 308, serial no. 4. Born January 17, baptized January 20, 1821. Witnesses: Jan Lustig and Cajsa Persdotter, Simonstorp Stom.

[136] Bolstad DFR 1812-45 (F:2), p. 79, serial no. missing. Dead August 1, buried August 7, 1824. Cause of death: dropsy.

[137] Gestad CHR 1819-24 (AI:10), p. 77. Missing in BBR.

[138] Bolstad DFR 1812-45 (F:2), p. 96, serial no. missing. Dead January 28, buried February 1, 1829. Cause of death: chest pain.

[139] Gestad BBR 1763-1833 (C:1), p. 350, serial no. missing. Born October 13, baptized October 15, 1826. Witnesses: Johan Lustig and Cajsa Persdotter, Simonstorp Stom.

[140] Bolstad DFR 1812-45 (F:2), p. 92, serial no. missing. Dead February 24, buried March 9, 1828. Cause of death: chest pain.

[141] Gestad BBR 1763-1833 (C:1), p. 365, serial no. missing. Born June 13, baptized June 19, 1829. Witnesses: Jan Lustig and Cajsa Persdotter, Simonstorp Stom.

[142] Gestad CHR 1824-29 (AI:11), p. 91.

[143] Gestad CHR 1829-35 (AI:12), p. 103.

[144] National Economic Maps, Elfsborg Province, Sundal Judicial District – eastern part, 1895. Map room, Stockholm University.

[145] Bolstad RR 1826-44 (B:2), p. 93, year 1835, serial no. 19 and Brålanda RR 1821-36 (B:1), p. 81, year 1835, serial no. 13.

[146] Brålanda RR 1837-48 (B:2), p. 8, year 1837, serial no. 19 and Bolstad RR 1826-44 (B:2), p. 100, serial no. 22.

[147] Gestad CHR 1836-41 (AI:13), p. 9.

[148] Bolstad CHR 1836-42 (AI:11), p. 70.

[149] Bolstad CHR 1836-42 (AI:11), p. 63.

[150] Bolstad CHR 1836-42 (AI:11), p. 166.

[151] Bolstad CHR 1836-42 (AI:11), p. 70.

[152] Gestad CHR 1836-41 (AI:13), p. 245, and Bolstad CHR 1836-42 (AI:11), p. 115.

[153] Bolstad RR 1826-44 (B:2), p. 45, year 1841, serial no. 21 and 22, and Västra Tunhem RR 1808-48 (B:2), p. 182, year 1841, serial no. 38.

[154] Gestad CHR 1836-41 (AI:13), p. 9, and Bolstad DFR 1812-45 (F:2), p. 165, serial no. missing. The boy stillborn July 3, buried July 10, 1842. Maja Stina dead July 19, 1842, according to CHR but missing in DFR.

[155] Citation from the entailment declaration taken from *Onsjö Manor – Kulturhistorisk undersökning av byggnader*, Älvsborg Provinces Historical Society, not dated, p. 15.

[156] National Economic Maps, Elfsborg Province, Väne Judicial District, 1895. Map room, Stockholm University.

[157] Sjögren, Bengt O. T.: *Porträttsamlingen på Onsjö* from Vänersborgs Söners Gille yearbook 1983.

[158] Vassända-Naglum CHR 1840-45 (AI:6), p. 77.

[159] In Sweden, the monetary unit riksdaler was replaced by crowns in 1873.

[160] Wenersborgs Weckoblad, No. 21, May 26, 1842, p. 1. By mistake this issue of the paper was printed with the same heading as the previous issue, that is No. 20, May 19, 1842.

[161] Daniel Thunberg was a Swedish passenger ship that frequented the distance Stockholm – Gothenburg via the Göta Canal during the years 1835-1850.

[162] Västra Tunhem BMR 1818-44 (E-1), p. 186, year 1835, serial no. 14.

[163] Vänersborg DFR 1838-60 (E:1), p. 527. Dead in Linköping May 5, buried May 12, 1838. Cause of death: cold.

[164] Grave Register for Linköping Old Cemetery 1811-1996 (D III:1).

[165] *Onsjö Manor – Kulturhistorisk undersökning av byggnader*, Älvsborg Provinces Historical Society, not dated, p. 47.

[166] Vassända-Naglum RR 1841-65 (B:1), year 1841, serial no. 61 and 62.

[167] Vassända-Naglum CHR 1840-45 (AI:6), p. 77.

[168] National Economic Maps, Elfsborg Province, Väne Judicial District, 1895. Map room, Stockholm University.

[169] Photo: Ingrid Hällgren Skoglund, 2017.

[170] Gärdhem BBR 1780-1818 (C:4), p. 41, serial no. 61. Born September 20, baptized September 21, 1795. Witnesses: Olof Thomaeson, Annika Pehrsdotter, Annika Thomaedotter.

[171] TR 1642-1820 Älvsborg Province, year 1795, p. 29.

[172] Väne-Åsaka CHR 1813-18 (AI:1), p. 480 and 479. Västra Tunhem CHR 1813-18 (AI:1), p. 37.

[173] Västra Tunhem CHR 1813-18 (AI:1), p. 67.

[174] Västra Tunhem CHR 1813-18 (AI:1), p. 65.

[175] Västra Tunhem BMR 1780-1817 (C:3), p. 315, year 1816, serial no. 20.

[176] Norra Björke BBR 1702-79 (C:2), p. 48, year 1742. Neither birth date nor witnesses are noted.

[177] Norra Björke BMR 1702-1779 (C:2), p. 322, year 1774.

[178] TR 1642-1820 Älvsborg Province, year 1744, p. 12.

[179] Norra Björke BBR 1702-79 (C:2), p. 44. Born February 5, 1738. No witnesses are noted.

[180] TR 1642-1820 Älvsborg Province, year 1744 p. 11.

[181] TR 1642-1820 Älvsborg Province, year 1761, p. 19.

[182] Norra Björke BMR 1702-1779 (C:2), p. 315, year 1760.

[183] TR 1642-1820 Älvsborg Province, year 1766, p. 17.

[184] TR 1642-1820 Älvsborg Province, year 1767, p. 18.

[185] TR 1642-1820 Älvsborg Province, year 1771, p. 17.

[186] Norra Björke BBR 1702-1779 (C:2), p. 91. Born February 12, baptized February 15, 1767. Witnesses: Bengt Månsson, Sven Nilsson, Kerstin Andersdotter, and Britta Jonsdotter.

[187] General Muster Roll Västgöta-Dals Regiment 1767-73, p. 211. Major/Väne Company, Third Corporalship, soldier no. 365.

[188] Norra Björke DFR 1702-79 (C:2), p. 451, and TR 1642-1820 Älvsborg Province, year 1774, p. 22. Dead December 9, buried December 13, 1772. Cause of death: dysentery.

[189] Norra Björke BMR 1702-1779 (C:2), p. 322, year 1774.

[190] Norra Björke BBR 1702-79 (C:2), p. 107. Born October 9, baptized October 10, 1775. Witnesses: Olof Böngren, Hans Lundborg, Maja Larsdotter, and Lena Andersdotter.

[191] Norra Björke DFR 1702-1779 (C:2), p. 456. Strangely enough, Pär is noted as dead twice in the DFR: 1) Dead January 11, buried January 14, 1775. Cause of death: disease. 2) Dead March 8, buried March 10, 1775. Cause of death not stated. Name, parents, and dwelling place are identical both times.

[192] General Muster Roll Västgöta-Dal Regiment 1778-85, picture 84, p. 155. Major/Väne Company, Third Corporalship, no. 365.

[193] General Muster Roll Västgöta-Dal Regiment 1778-85, picture 392. Major/Väne Company, Third Corporalship, soldier no. 365.

[194] TR 1642-1820 Älvsborg Province, year 1779, p. 19.

[195] General Muster Roll Västgöta-Dal Regiment 1778-85, picture 392. Major/Väne Company, Third Corporalship, soldier no. 365.

[196] Uddevalla RR 1786-1812 (B:1), p. 10, year 1787, serial no. 230.

[197] Tanum RR 1779-1852 (B:1), p. 7, year 1782, serial no. 122.

[198] General Muster Roll Bohuslän Regiment 1783, picture 288. Tanum Company, First Corporalship, soldier no. 32.

[199] Västra Tunhem BBR 1780-1817 (C:3), p. 11. Born November 1, baptized November 2, 1784. Witnesses: Anders Hindriksson, Pehr Olofsson, Elin Svensdotter, and Maja Andersdotter.

[200] Västra Tunhem BMR 1780-1817 (C:3), p. 341, year 1787, serial no. 15.

[201] National Law of 1734, Marriage Law, Chapter 13, § 4.

[202] Västra Tunhem BBR 1702-1780 (C:2), p. 203. Born April 2, baptized April 3, 1763. Witnesses: Måns Torstensson, Anders Torbjörnsson, Karin Aronsdotter, Kierstin Andersdotter.

[203] TR 1642-1820 Älvsborg Province, year 1755 p. 507, year 1760 p. 8, year 1780 p. 10, year 1782 p. 10, year 1783 p. 9, year 1784 p. 10, year 1785 p. 9.

[204] Uddevalla RR 1786-1812 (B:1), p. 10, year 1787, serial no. 230.

[205] Uddevalla BBR 1775-95 (C:5), p. 151. Born August 27, baptized August 28, 1787. Witnesses of the father: the worker Anders Torbjörnsson, dito Bengt Kamp, the farmhand Olof Olsson. Witnesses of the mother: the widow Kirstin Celin, the miller Berndt Collin's wife Elin Björnsdotter, the maid Elin Eriksdotter.

[206] Västra Tunhem BMR 1780-1817 (C:3), p. 343, year 1787, serial no. 39.

[207] Uddevalla DFR 1775-95 (C:5), p. 397. Dead June 19, buried June 24, 1788. Cause of death: smallpox.

[208] General Muster Roll Bohuslän Regiment 1788, p. 293. Tanum Company, First Corporalship, soldier no. 32.

[209] Uddevalla RR 1786-1812 (B:1), p. 17, year 1789, serial no. 137.

[210] Västra Tunhem BBR 1780-1817 (C:3), p. 56. Born August 2, 1789. Witnesses: Lars Andersson, Jonas Andersson, Maja Catharina Wetterin, Karin Andersdotter.

[211] Västra Tunhem BBR 1780-1817 (C:3), p. 86. Born and baptized August 5, 1791. Witnesses: Berit Larsdotter, Annika Jonsdotter, Brita Jonsdotter.

[212] Norra Björke BBR 1780-1817 (C:3), p. 11, serial no. 14. Born September 26, baptized September 27, 1793. Witnesses: Anders Hindricsson, Lars Björkman, Catharina Andersdotter, Annika Pehrsdotter. The place of birth can be found in Västra Tunhem CHR 1813-18 (AI:1), p. 115.

[213] Carlén, Johan Gabriel: *Handbok i svensk lagfarenhet*, Stockholm 1843.

[214] Västra Tunhem CHR 1813-18 (AI:1), p. 115.

[215] Västra Tunhem BMR 1818-44 (E:1), p. 29, year 1820, serial no. 6.

[216] Västra Tunhem CHR 1818-28 (AI:2), p. 154.

[217] Västra Tunhem DFR 1818-49 (C:4), p. 239. Dead April 15, buried April 20, 1828. Cause of death: dropsy.

[218] Västra Tunhem DFR 1818-49 (C:4), p. 242. Dead December 13, buried December 21, 1828. Cause of death: old age.

[219] Färgelanda CHR 1795-1801 (AI:6), p. 1.

[220] Färgelanda CHR 1802-06 (AI:7), p. 1. Färgelanda CHR 1806-10 (AI:8), p. 1. Färgelanda CHR 1810-14 (AI-9), p. 4

[221] Färgelanda CHR 1810-14 (AI:9), p. 135

[222] Färgelanda RR 1810-30 (B:1), picture 78, year 1813, serial no. 102. Västra Tunhem RR 1808-48 (B:2), p. 23, year 1813, serial no. 524.

[223] Västra Tunhem CHR 1813-18 (AI:1), p. 115.

[224] Västra Tunhem BBR 1818-49 (C:4), p. 20. Born and baptized February 16, 1820. Witnesses: Anders Andersson, the wife Kerstin Svensdotter of Bryggum, the maid Maija Andersdotter of Prästgården.

[225] Västra Tunhem CHR 1813-18 (AI:1), p. 129.

[226] Västra Tunhem CHR 1813-18 (AI:1), p. 35.

[227] Västra Tunhem CHR 1813-18 (AI:1), p. 65.

[228] Västra Tunhem CHR 1813-18 (AI:1), p. 115.

[229] Västra Tunhem BBR 1780-1817 (C:3), p. 255. Born and baptized September 18, 1817. Witnesses: Pehr Hallström, Kerstin Ericsdotter, Ingrid Andersdotter

[230] Västra Tunhem CHR 1818-28 (AI:2), p. 75.

[231] Västra Tunhem BBR 1818-49 (C:4), p. 20. Born and baptized February 16, 1820. Witnesses: Anders Andersson with his wife Kerstin Svensdotter, Bryggum, the maid Maja Andersdotter, Prästgården.

[232] Västra Tunhem BBR 1818-49 (C:4), p. 30. Born and baptized April 16, 1822. Witnesses: Anders Bengtsson with his wife Greta Jonasdotter.

[233] Västra Tunhem BBR 1818-49 (C:4), p. 40. Born and baptized January 6, 1824. Witnesses: Anders Bengtsson with his wife Greta Jonasdotter of Bryggum Manor.

[234] Västra Tunhem BBR 1818-49 (C:4), p. 52. Born November 14, baptized November 15, 1825. Witnesses: Greta Jonasdotter with her husband Anders Bengtsson.

[235] Västra Tunhem DFR 1818-49 (C:4), p. 263. Dead November 29, buried December 4, 1836. Cause of death: measles.

[236] Västra Tunhem BBR 1818-49 (C:4), p. 73. Born October 18, baptized October 19, 1828. Witnesses: Greta Jonasdotter and Johannes Andersson, Bryggum.

[237] Västra Tunhem DFR 1818-49 (C:4), p. 244. Dead January 4, buried January 11, 1829. Cause of death: whooping cough.

[238] Västra Tunhem BBR 1818-49 (C:4), p. 87. Born and baptized June 10, 1830. Witnesses: Anna Bengtsdotter with her husband Jonas Torstenson, Berget.

[239] Västra Tunhem DFR 1850-72 (C:5), p. 25. Dead September 24, buried September 28, 1856. Cause of death: dropsy.

[240] Västra Tunhem BBR 1818-49 (C:4), p. 103. Born January 30, baptized February 1, 1833. Witnesses: The widow Greta Jansdotter of Jordahla, the cottager Olaus Andersson, Aleklev.

[241] Västra Tunhem DFR 1850-72 (C:5), p. 36. Dead December 18, buried December 24, 1859. Cause of death: tuberculoses and wasting.

[242] Västra Tunhem BBR 1818-49 (C:4), p. 126. Born December 15, baptized December 16, 1835. Witnesses: The widow Britta Hallström and Lars Jonsson, Lunden.

[243] Västra Tunhem DFR 1818-49 (C:4), p. 263. Dead November 23, buried December 11, 1836. Cause of death not stated. The pastor has written Inga Stina but should it be Inga Beata.

[244] Västra Tunhem BBR 1818-49 (C:4), p. 142. Born November 22, baptized November 23, 1837. Witnesses: Anna Bengtsdotter, Berget, Greta Jonasdotter, Måsen, Jacob Linnarsson, Bastebäcken.

[245] Västra Tunhem BBR 1818-49 (C:4), p. 142. Born and baptized November 23, 1837. Witnesses: Anna Bengtsdotter, Berget, Greta Jonasdotter, Måsen, Jacob Linnarsson, Bastebäcken.

[246] Västra Tunhem DFR 1850-72 (C:5), p. 14. Dead February 20, buried February 27, 1853. Cause of death: dropsy.

[247] Västra Tunhem CHR 1829-38 (AI:3), p. 83.

[248] Västra Tunhem CHR 1829-38 (AI:3), p. 76.

[249] Västra Tunhem RR 1808-48 (B:2), p. 297, serial no. 105. Vänersborg RR 1831-52 (B:1), year 1834, serial no. 76.

[250] Vassända-Naglums CHR 1829-36 (AI:3), p. 140. Vassända-Naglums CHR 1836-40 (AI:5), p. 3.

[251] Vänersborg RR 1831-52 (B:1), year 1837, serial no. 110. Västra Tunhem RR 1808-48 (B:2), p. 161, serial no. 31. Västra Tunhem CHR 1829-38 (AI:3), p. 73.

[252] Västra Tunhem CHR 1838-53 (AI:4), p. 96 and p. 477.

[253] Västra Tunhem RR 1808-48 (B:2), p. 333, serial no. 30.

[254] Tidning för Wenersborgs stad och län, No. 22, May 29, 1849, p. 2.

[255] Västra Tunhem CHR 1838-53 (AI:4), p. 198.

[256] Västra Tunhem DFR 1850-72 (C:5), p. 42, serial no. 25. Dead May 31, buried June 3, 1861. Cause of death not stated.

[257] Västra Tunhem CHR 1853-67 (AI-5), p. 134.

[258] Fuxerna DFR 1895-1924 (F:2), p. 94, serial no. 12. Dead April 7, buried April 13, 1914. Cause of death: acute pneumonia.

[259] Vassända-Naglum CHR 1840-45 (AI:6), p. 77.

[260] Vassända-Naglum RR 1841-65 (B:1), year 1842, serial no. 22 and 28 respectively. For Sven Andersson is erroneously noted that he moves to Tunhem.

[261] Bolstad RR 1826-44 (B:2), p. 114, serial no. 2 and 7 respectively.

[262] Gestad BMR 1842, last pages in RR 1806-26 (B:2), serial no. 14.

[263] Gestad CHR 1842-46 (AI:14), p. 9.

[264] Bolstad RR 1826-44 (B:2), p. 119, serial no. 2 and 3.

[265] Gestad CHR 1842-46 (AI:14), p. 9.

[266] Gestad CHR 1846-51 (AI:15), s.108, p. 9, p. 84 and Gestad CHR 1851-55 (AI:16), p. 96.

[267] Gestad RR 1845-60 (B:2), p. 117, serial no. 6, and Vänersnäs RR 1827-55 (B:2), p. 105, serial no. 28.

[268] Vänersnäs CHR 1851-61 (AI-3), p. 61, and Vänersnäs CHR 1851-61 (AI-3) p. 164.

[269] Vänersnäs RR 1827-55 (B-2) p. 117 serial no. 14.

[270] Gestad CHR 1851-55 (AI:16), p. 12, and Gestad DFR 1845-60 (F:1), p. 18. Dead March 2, buried March 13, 1853. Cause of death not stated.

[271] Gestad CHR 1856-60 (AI:17), p. 9.

[272] Gestad DFR 1861-1894 (F:2), p. 1, serial no. 9. Dead February 5, buried February 10, 1861. Cause of death not stated.

[273] Västra Tunhem RR 1808-48, p. 190, serial no. 48 and 79.

[274] *Historisk statistik för Sverige II – Väderlek, lantmäteri, jordbruk, skogsbruk, fiske t.o.m. år 1955*, Statistics Sweden, Stockholm, 1959. Table D 4, p. 16. http://hdl.handle.net/2077/855

[275] *Tidning för Wenersborgs Stad och Län*, April 1, 1870.

[276] Land Survey Board Archive, Västra Tunhems Parish, Malöga, Legal Redistribution, 1836.

[277] Västra Tunhem CHR 1838-53 (AI:4), p. 160.

[278] Västra Tunhem CHR 1838-53 (AI:4), p. 160. Can not be found in BBR.

[279] Västra Tunhem BBR 1818-49 (C:4), p. 188. Born February 9, baptized February 10, 1846. Witnesses: Andreas Andersson and his wife of Pehrsgården.

[280] Västra Tunhem BBR 1818-49 (C:4), p. 201. Born October 11, baptized October 12, 1847. Witnesses: Gunnar Olofsson and Britta Nilsdotter of Pehrsgården.

[281] *Svenska adelns ättartavlor, Avdelning 1. Abrahamsson – Granfelt*, red. Gabriel Anrep, P. A. Norstedt & Sons, Stockholm 1858, p. 673. http://runeberg.org/anrep/1/0681.html

[282] Västra Tunhem CHR 1838-53 (AI:4), p. 259.

[283] *Vårt lands kulturhistoria i skildringar och bilder – Vid 1800-talets mitt*, red. Ewert Wrangel, 9th volume, Magazine Publisher Allhem, Malmö 1939, p. 267. http://runeberg.org/svfolket/9/0307.html

[284] Västra Tunhem DFR 1850-72 (C:5), p. 3. Dead April 5, buried April 14, 1850. Cause of death: measles.

[285] Västra Tunhem DFR 1850-72 (C:5), p. 6. Dead January 28, buried February 2, 1851. Cause of death: drowned by accident.

[286] http://magasin.kb.se:8080/searchinterface/title.jsp?id=kb:70301&offset=100

[287] Västra Tunhem CHR 1853-67 (AI:5), p. 249.

[288] Västra Tunhem BMR 1848-70 (E:3), p. 44-45.

[289] Bolstad BBR 1763-1833 (C:1), p. 259, serial no. 9. Born February 11, baptized February 14, 1812. Witnesses: Bengt Nilsson and his wife Britta Olofsdotter of Norra Hagen. Here Muggerud is erroneously said to be located under Norra Hagen.

[290] Bolstad CHR 1809-13 (AI:6), p. 181.

[291] Bolstad CHR 1809-13 (AI:6), p. 161.

[292] Bolstad CHR 1814-18 (AI:7), p. 193 and Bolstad DFR 1812-45 (F:2), p. 15, serial no. 25. Dead May 23, buried May 30, 1814. Cause of death: fever.

[293] Bolstad BMR 1763-1840 (E:1), p. 249, year 1818, serial no. 25.

[294] Bolstad CHR 1819-24 (AI:8), p. 165.

[295] Bolstad CHR 1824-28 (AI:9), p. 45.

[296] Bolstad CHR 1824-28 (AI-9), p. 93.

[297] Bolstad CHR 1824-28 (AI:9), p. 45, 47, 21 and 111. Bolstad CHR 1829-35 (AI:10), p. 131, 34, 50, 152 and 13. Bolstad CHR 1836-42 (AI:11), p. 11 and 156.

[298] Bolstad RR 1826-44 (B:2), p. 33, serial no. 8, and Västra Tunhem RR 1808-48 (B:2), p. 163, serial no. 51.

[299] Innovatum Photo Archive, photo no. TB-1116.

[300] Gärdhem CHR 1829-38 (AI:3), p. 483.

[301] Gärdhem CHR 1838-53 (AI:4), p. 555.

[302] Västra Tunhem BMR 1818-44 (E:1), p. 222-223, year 1839, serial no. 19.

[303] Gärdhem CHR 1838-53 (AI:4), p. 544, and Gärdhem CHR 1843-54 (AI:5), p. 168 and 88.

[304] Gärdhem BBR 1818-43 (C:5), p. 198. Born June 6, baptized June 7 1840. Witnesses: Ehfraim Andersson and his wife Inga Petersdotter, Trollhättan.

[305] Gärdhem BBR 1818-43 (C:5), p. 212. Born April 13, baptized April 14, 1842. Witnesses: Carl W Pettersson and his wife Maria Magnedotter, Trollhättan.

[306] Gärdhem BBR 1843-57 (C:6), p. 12. Born June 8, baptized June 9, 1844. Witnesses: Johan Phersson and his wife Charlotta Hansdotter, Trollhättan.

[307] Gärdhem DFR 1843-57 (C:6), p. 24. Dead May 4, buried May 9, 1852. Cause of death: smallpox.

[308] Gärdhem BBR 1843-57 (C:6), p. 38. Born and baptized July 24, 1847. Witnesses: The tailor Olaus Svensson and his wife Inga Lena Svensdotter, Trollhättan.

[309] Gärdhem BBR 1843-57 (C:6), p. 70. Born May 13, baptized May 14, 1850. Witnesses: The tailor Olaus Svensson and his wife Inga Lena Svensdotter, Trollhättan.

[310] Innovatum Photo Archive, photo no. TB-152-089.

[311] Gärdhem DFR 1843-57 (C:6), p. 15. Dead October 23, buried October 25. Cause of death: cholera. In Gärdhem Parish 40 persons died of cholera between October 3 and November 18, 1850, 11 persons between August 28 and October 6, 1853, and 38 persons between September 25 and November 8, 1857.

[312] Gärdhem CHR 1843-54 (AI:5), p. 168 (far down on the page).

[313] Gärdhem CHR 1838-53 (AI:4), p. 682, and Gärdhem CHR 1854-60 (AI:8), p. 487 and 31.

[314] http://bibblansvarar.se/sv/svar/hur-lange-fick-man-jobba-i-186

[315] https://sv.wikipedia.org/wiki/%C3%85ttatimMarchdagen

[316] Västra Tunhem BMR 1848-70 (E:3), p. 44-45.

[317] Västra Tunhem CHR 1853-67 (AI:5), p. 249.

[318] Gärdhem CHR 1854-60 (AI:8), p. 31.

[319] Gärdhem CHR 1854-60 (AI:8), p. 115, 523 and 59.
Trollhättan CHR 1863-68 (AI:1), p. 209.

[320] Trollhättan RR 1860-87 (BI:1), year 1861, serial no. 29, and Gothenburg Domkyrko PR 1861-83 (AIa:9), p. 690.

[321] Trollhättan RR 1860-87 (BI:1), year 1863, serial no. 16.

[322] Trollhättan RR 1860-87 (BI:1), year 1862, serial no. 61. Moved to "Gust(af) Ad(olf)" = Vassända-Naglum.
Vassända-Naglum RR 1841-65 (B:1), year 1862, serial no. 96.

[323] Vassända-Naglum CHR 1856-69 (AI:10), p. 75.

[324] Vänersborg CHR 1856-69 (AI:19), p. 80.

[325] Vänersborg RR 1853-86 (B:2), year 1864, serial no. 98 and Gothenburg Domkyrko PR 1861-83 (AIa:9), p. 719.

[326] Gothenburg Domkyrko RR 1861-79 (B:7), year 1868, picture 473 and Vänersborg RR 1853-86 (B:2), year 1868, serial no. 135.

[327] Vänersborg CHR 1856-69 (AI:21), p. 346.

[328] Vänersborg RR 1853-86 (B:2), year 1869, serial no. 37.

[329] Gothenburg Domkyrko BBR 1872-77 (C:13), picture 36, serial no. 453. Born May 8, baptized May 24, 1872. Witnesses: The wife Maria Calberg, the wife Charlotta Eliasson.

[330] Gothenburg Domkyrko PR 1866-83 (AIa:10), p. 760, and Gothenburg Domkyrko RR 1861-79 (B:7), year 1872, picture 371.

[331] National census 1885 for 0301 Kristiania kjøpstad, p. 7925.

[332] Trollhättan DFR 1860-85 (FI:1), p. 40, serial no. 33. Dead October 18, buried October 23, 1864. Cause of death: Pneumonia c. hepatitide.

[333] Trollhättan CHR 1863-68 (AI:1), p. 32. Mossen No. 16. Starting with this register, Cajsa is spelled Kajsa.

[334] Royal bylaw regarding changes of certain parts of the legal rules about marriage rights and inheritance rights, Stockholm 19 May 1845.

[335] Trollhättan RR 1860-87 (BI:1), year 1865, serial no. 78.

[336] Trollhättan RR 1860-87 (BI:1), year 1866, serial no. 42.

[337] Trollhättan CHR 1863-68 (AI:1), p. 87.

[338] Trollhättan CHR 1868-76 (AI:2), p. 467

[339] Andersson, Inga-Lill: *Fattighus*,
http://docplayer.se/9886566-Fattighus-inga-lill-andersson.html

[340] Trollhättan CHR 1868-76 (AI:2) p. 467,
Trollhättan CHR 1877-84 (AI:4), p. 649,
Trollhättan CHR 1877-84 (AI:3), p. 170,
Trollhättan CHR 1884-90 (AI:5), p. 202 and 216,
Trollhättan CHR 1884-90 (AI:6), p. 425,
Trollhättan CHR 1891-94 (AI:8), p. 451,
Trollhättan CR 1895-99 (AIIaa:3), p. 742 and
Trollhättan CR 1900-08 (AIIaa:6), p. 79.

[341] Trollhättan CR 1900-08 (AIIaa:5) p. 170.

[342] Trollhättan CHR 1877-84 (AI:3), p. 170.

[343] Trollhättan BMR 1860-94 (EI:1), p. 55, year 1868, serial no. 12. Banns
June 28, wedding August 2 1868. Witnesses: Johan Cederström with wife.

[344] Trollhättan BBR 1860-76 (CI:1), p. 164, serial no. 74. Born September 9,
baptized September 13, 1868. Witnesses: Anders Magnus Persson with
wife.

[345] Ödsmål BBR 1839-61 (C:3), p. 7. Born December 2, baptized December
4, 1839. Witnesses: Herman Johansson and Ingeborg Olsdotter of Pan-
neröd.

[346] Ödsmål CHR 1831-36 (AI:6), p. 34.

[347] Ucklum CHR 1831-37 (AI:6), p. 93, 96 and 13.

[348] Norum CHR 1836-40 (AI:5), p. 17.

[349] Norum RR 1821-1872 (B:1), p. 18, year 1839, serial no. 22.

[350] Ödsmål CHR 1838-40 (AI:8), p. 20.

[351] Navy Archive of Seamen Companies 1754-1803, picture 172, year 1803,
and 1808-1822, picture 380, year 1821.

[352] Ödsmål BMR 1766-1839 (C:2), p. 8, year 1766.

[353] Ödsmål BMR 1839-1861 (E:1), p. 50 f, year 1848, serial no. 9.
Ödsmål BMR 1839-1861 (C:3), p. 316, year 1848.

[354] Ödsmål CHR 1850-55 (AI:12), p. 97.

[355] Ödsmål BBR 1839-61 (C:3), p. 70. Born March 24, baptized March 29,
1850. Witnesses: Gustaf Johansson, Sven Johansson under Bräcke. Gunil-
la Magnusdotter.

[356] Ödsmål DFR 1839-61 (C:3), p. 235. Dead April 18, buried April 24, 1855.
Cause of death not stated.

[357] Ödsmål BBR 1839-61 (C:3), p. 90. Born January 6, baptized January 9, 1853. Witnesses: Per Henricsson, Gustaf Andersson, Anna Andersdotter of Raden.

[358] Ödsmål BBR 1839-61 (C:3), p. 128. Born October 1, baptized October 4, 1857. Witnesses: Johan Simonsson under Raden, Beata Larsdotter.

[359] Ödsmål CHR 1850-55 (AI:12), p. 101.

[360] Ödsmål DFR 1839-61 (C:3), p. 234. Dead June 6, buried June 12, 1854. Cause of death not stated.

[361] Ödsmål CHR 1855-59 (AI:13), p. 72.

[362] Ödsmål CHR 1855-59 (AI:13), p. 105. Ödsmål CHR 1859-62 (AI:14), p. 99.

[363] Ödsmål CHR 1861-70 (AI:15), p. 151. Ödsmål RR 1836-72 (B:1), p. 55, year 1867, serial no. 7.

[364] Trollhättan RR 1860-87 (BI:1), year 1868, serial no. 48.

[365] Trollhättan BBR 1860-76 (CI:1), p. 164, serial no. 74. Born September 9, baptized September 13, 1868. Witnesses: Anders Magnus Persson with wife.

[366] Trollhättan BBR 1860-76 (CI:1), p. 190, serial no. 5. Born January 21, baptized January 30, 1870. Witnesses: J. F. Karlberg with wife.

[367] Trollhättan BBR 1860-76 (CI:1), p. 214, serial no. 19. Born March 2, baptized March 12, 1871. Witnesses: Emanuel Gren with wife.

[368] Trollhättan BBR 1860-76 (CI:1), p. 248, serial no. 68. Born October 8, baptized October 13, 1872. Witnesses: Emanuel Gren with wife.

[369] Trollhättan BBR 1860-76 (CI:1), p. 276, serial no. 86. Born November 22, baptized November 30, 1873. Witnesses: Bernard Andersson with wife.

[370] Trollhättan DFR 1860-85 (FI:1), p. 206, serial no. 37. Dead September 14, buried September 17, 1876. Cause of death: diphtheria.

[371] Trollhättan BBR 1860-76 (CI:1), p. 312, serial no. 33. Born April 1, baptized April 11, 1875. Witnesses: Johannes Roos with wife.

[372] Trollhättan BBR 1877-87 (CI:2), p. 68, serial no. 3. Born January 8, baptized January 19, 1879. Witnesses: Karl Jonsson with wife.

[373] Trollhättan BBR 1877-87 (CI:2), p. 114, serial no. 81. Born June 30, baptized July 11, 1880. Witnesses: Olaus Andersson with wife.

[374] Trollhättan BBR 1877-87 (CI:2), p. 152, serial no. 119. Born November 13, baptized November 27, 1881. Witnesses: Olaus Andersson with wife.

[375] Trollhättan BBR 1877-87 (CI:2), p. 222, serial no. 152. Born November 14, baptized December 23, 1883. Witnesses: Carl Hålberg (?) with wife.

[376] Trollhättan DFR 1886-94 (FI:2), p. 6, serial no. 19. Dead March 3, buried March 7, 1886. Cause of death: convulsiones.

[377] Trollhättan BBR 1877-87 (CI:2), p. 280, serial no. 75. Born May 21, baptized June 28, 1885. Witnesses: Melker Rådström with wife.

[378] Trollhättan BBR 1888-95 (CI:3), p. 14, serial no. 42. Born February 20, baptized April 15, 1888. Witness: Inga Brita Nilsdotter.

[379] Trollhättan BBR 1888-95 (CI:3), p. 130, serial no. 26. Born January 28, baptized March 8, 1890. Witnesses: A. F. Larsson with wife.

[380] Trollhättan CHR 1868-76 (AI:2) p. 248.

[381] Trollhättan CHR 1868-76 (AI:2), p. 185.

[382] Trollhättan CHR 1868-76 (AI:2), p. 166.

[383] Trollhättan CHR 1868-76 (AI:2), p. 239.

[384] Trollhättan CHR 1868-76 (AI:2), p. 235.
Trollhättan CHR 1877-84 (AI:4), p. 429.
Trollhättan CHR 1884-90 (AI:7), p. 625.

[385] Trollhättan RR 1888-95 (BI:2), year 1888, serial no. 68.
Karlsborg RR 1876-94 (B:3), picture 78, year 1888, serial no. 63.
Karlsborg CHR 1882-93 (AI:38), p. 18.
Karlsborg RR 1876-94 (B:4), picture 79, year 1890, serial no. 244.

[386] Trollhättan CHR 1891-94 (AI:9), p. 656.

[387] Trollhättan CR 1895-99 (AIIaa:1) p. 25.

[388] Trollhättan CHR 1884-90 (AI:7), p. 624.

[389] Trollhättan CHR 1877-84 (AI:4), p. 395.

[390] Trollhättan CHR 1868-76 (AI:2), p. 467.
Trollhättan CHR 1877-84 (AI:4), p. 649 and p. 170.
Trollhättan CHR 1884-90 (AI:5), p. 202 and p. 216.
Trollhättan CHR 1884-90 (AI:6), p. 425.

[391] Trollhättan CR 1895-99 (AIIaa:3), p. 742.
Trollhättan CR 1900-08 (AIIaa:6), p. 79.

[392] Trollhättan RR 1895-1908 (BI:3), p. 97, year 1902, serial no. 205.

[393] Trollhättan CR 1900-08 (AIIaa:5) p. 171.

[394] Trollhättan CR 1900-08 (AIIaa:5), p. 170.

[395] Trollhättan DFR 1895-07 (FI:3), p. 96, serial no. 45. Dead June 2, buried June 7, 1903. Cause of death: brain tumor.

[396] Trollhättan DFR 1895-07 (FI:3), p. 144, serial no. 77. Dead September 20, buried September 29, 1907. Cause of death: old age fading.

[397] Trollhättan DFR 1908-18 (FI:4), p. 11, serial no. 104. Dead September 13, buried September 20, 1908. Cause of death: stroke.

[398] https://sv.wikipedia.org/wiki/Svenska_efternamn

[399] Trollhättan CHR 1884-90 (AI-5), p. 216.

[400] Trollhättan CR 1900-08 (AIIaa-5), p. 170.

[401] Norum CHR 1836-40 (AI:5), p. 17.

[402] Sundals Judicial District Estate Inventories 1798, p. 1 ff.

[403] Sundals Judicial District Estate Inventories 1804-05, p. 15 ff.

[404] Väne Judicial District Estate Inventories 1863-70 (FII:17), p. 651 ff.

[405] Flundre, Väne and Björke Judicial District Estate Inventories 1903 (FII:8), picture 3960 f.

[406] Gothenburg Cathedral Chapter Archive, Marriage documents (divorce decisions), 1796-1798, picture 141 ff.

CPSIA information can be obtained
at www.ICGtesting.com
Printed in the USA
LVHW02s0335051217
558684LV00030B/2271/P